The Law School Admission Council (LSAC) is a nonprofit corporation that provides unique, state-of-the-art admission products and services to ease the admission process for law schools and their applicants worldwide. Currently, 218 law schools in the United States, Canada, and Australia are members of the Council and benefit from LSAC's services.

ISBN-13: 978-0-9846360-8-2

TABLE OF CONTENTS

INTRODUCTION TO THE LSAT

The Law School Admission Test is a half-day standardized test required for admission to all ABA-approved law schools, most Canadian law schools, and many other law schools. It consists of five 35-minute sections of multiple-choice questions. Four of the five sections contribute to the test taker's score. These sections include one Reading Comprehension section, one Analytical Reasoning section, and two Logical Reasoning sections. The unscored section, commonly referred to as the variable section, typically is used to pretest new test questions or to preequate new test forms. The placement of this section in the LSAT will vary. A 35-minute writing sample is administered at the end of the test. The writing sample is not scored by LSAC, but copies are sent to all law schools to which you apply. The score scale for the LSAT is 120 to 180.

The LSAT is designed to measure skills considered essential for success in law school: the reading and comprehension of complex texts with accuracy and insight; the organization and management of information and the ability to draw reasonable inferences from it; the ability to think critically; and the analysis and evaluation of the reasoning and arguments of others.

The LSAT provides a standard measure of acquired reading and verbal reasoning skills that law schools can use as one of several factors in assessing applicants.

For up-to-date information about LSAC's services, go to our website, LSAC.org.

SCORING

Your LSAT score is based on the number of questions you answer correctly (the raw score). There is no deduction for incorrect answers, and all questions count equally. In other words, there is no penalty for guessing.

Test Score Accuracy—Reliability and Standard Error of Measurement

Candidates perform at different levels on different occasions for reasons quite unrelated to the characteristics of a test itself. The accuracy of test scores is best described by the use of two related statistical terms: reliability and standard error of measurement.

Reliability is a measure of how consistently a test measures the skills being assessed. The higher the reliability coefficient for a test, the more certain we can be that test takers would get very similar scores if they took the test again.

LSAC reports an internal consistency measure of reliability for every test form. Reliability can vary from 0.00 to 1.00, and a test with no measurement error would have a reliability coefficient of 1.00 (never attained in practice). Reliability coefficients for past LSAT forms have ranged from .90 to .95, indicating a high degree of consistency for these tests. LSAC expects the reliability of the LSAT to continue to fall within the same range.

LSAC also reports the amount of measurement error associated with each test form, a concept known as the standard error of measurement (SEM). The SEM, which is usually about 2.6 points, indicates how close a test taker's observed score is likely to be to his or her true score. True scores are theoretical scores that would be obtained from perfectly reliable tests with no measurement error—scores never known in practice.

Score bands, or ranges of scores that contain a test taker's true score a certain percentage of the time, can be derived using the SEM. LSAT score bands are constructed by adding and subtracting the (rounded) SEM to and from an actual LSAT score (e.g., the LSAT score, plus or minus 3 points). Scores near 120 or 180 have asymmetrical bands. Score bands constructed in this manner will contain an individual's true score approximately 68 percent of the time.

Measurement error also must be taken into account when comparing LSAT scores of two test takers. It is likely that small differences in scores are due to measurement error rather than to meaningful differences in ability. The standard error of score differences provides some guidance as to the importance of differences between two scores. The standard error of score differences is approximately 1.4 times larger than the standard error of measurement for the individual scores.

Thus, a test score should be regarded as a useful but approximate measure of a test taker's abilities as measured by the test, not as an exact determination of his or her abilities. LSAC encourages law schools to examine the range of scores within the interval that probably contains the test taker's true score (e.g., the test taker's score band) rather than solely interpret the reported score alone.

Adjustments for Variation in Test Difficulty

All test forms of the LSAT reported on the same score scale are designed to measure the same abilities, but one test form may be slightly easier or more difficult than another. The scores from different test forms are made comparable through a statistical procedure known as equating. As a result of equating, a given scaled score earned on different test forms reflects the same level of ability.

Research on the LSAT

Summaries of LSAT validity studies and other LSAT research can be found in member law school libraries and at LSAC.org.

To Inquire About Test Questions

If you find what you believe to be an error or ambiguity in a test question that affects your response to the question, contact LSAC by e-mail: LSATTS@LSAC.org, or write to Law School Admission Council, Test Development Group, PO Box 40, Newtown, PA 18940-0040.

HOW THIS PREPTEST DIFFERS FROM AN ACTUAL LSAT

This PrepTest is made up of the scored sections and writing sample from the actual disclosed LSAT administered in June 2013. However, it does not contain the extra, variable section that is used to pretest new test items of one of the three multiple-choice question types. The three multiple-choice question types may be in a different order in an actual LSAT than in this PrepTest. This is because the order of these question types is intentionally varied for each administration of the test.

THE THREE LSAT MULTIPLE-CHOICE QUESTION TYPES

The multiple-choice questions that make up most of the LSAT reflect a broad range of academic disciplines and are intended to give no advantage to candidates from a particular academic background.

The five sections of the test contain three different question types. The following material presents a general discussion of the nature of each question type and some strategies that can be used in answering them.

Analytical Reasoning Questions

Analytical Reasoning questions are designed to assess the ability to consider a group of facts and rules, and, given those facts and rules, determine what could or must be true. The specific scenarios associated with these questions are usually unrelated to law, since they are intended to be accessible to a wide range of test takers. However, the skills tested parallel those involved in determining what could or must be the case given a set of regulations, the terms of a contract, or the facts of a legal case in relation to the law. In Analytical Reasoning questions, you are asked to reason deductively from a set of statements and rules or principles that describe relationships among persons, things, or events.

Analytical Reasoning questions appear in sets, with each set based on a single passage. The passage used for each set of questions describes common ordering relationships or grouping relationships, or a combination of both types of relationships. Examples include scheduling employees for work shifts, assigning instructors to class sections, ordering tasks according to priority, and distributing grants for projects.

Analytical Reasoning questions test a range of deductive reasoning skills. These include:

- Comprehending the basic structure of a set of relationships by determining a complete solution to the problem posed (for example, an acceptable seating arrangement of all six diplomats around a table)

- Reasoning with conditional ("if-then") statements and recognizing logically equivalent formulations of such statements

- Inferring what could be true or must be true from given facts and rules

- Inferring what could be true or must be true from given facts and rules together with new information in the form of an additional or substitute fact or rule

- Recognizing when two statements are logically equivalent in context by identifying a condition or rule that could replace one of the original conditions while still resulting in the same possible outcomes

Analytical Reasoning questions reflect the kinds of detailed analyses of relationships and sets of constraints that a law student must perform in legal problem solving. For example, an Analytical Reasoning passage might describe six diplomats being seated around a table, following certain rules of protocol as to who can sit where. You, the test taker, must answer questions about the logical implications of given and new information. For example, you may be asked who can sit between diplomats X and Y, or who cannot sit next to X if W sits next to Y. Similarly, if you were a student in law school, you might be asked to analyze a scenario involving a set of particular circumstances and a set of governing rules in the form of constitutional provisions, statutes, administrative codes, or prior rulings that have been upheld. You might then be asked to determine the legal options in the scenario: what is required given the scenario, what is permissible given the scenario, and what is prohibited given the scenario. Or you might be asked to develop a "theory" for the case: when faced with an incomplete set of facts about the case, you must fill in the picture based on what is implied by the facts that are known. The problem could be elaborated by the addition of new information or hypotheticals.

No formal training in logic is required to answer these questions correctly. Analytical Reasoning questions are intended to be answered using knowledge, skills, and reasoning ability generally expected of college students and graduates.

Suggested Approach

Some people may prefer to answer first those questions about a passage that seem less difficult and then those that seem more difficult. In general, it is best to finish one passage before starting on another, because much time can be lost in returning to a passage and reestablishing familiarity with its relationships. However, if you are having great difficulty on one particular set of questions and are spending too much time on them, it may be to your advantage to skip that set of questions and go on to the next passage, returning to the problematic set of questions after you have finished the other questions in the section.

Do not assume that because the conditions for a set of questions look long or complicated, the questions based on those conditions will be especially difficult.

Read the passage carefully. Careful reading and analysis are necessary to determine the exact nature of the relationships involved in an Analytical Reasoning passage. Some relationships are fixed (for example, P and R must always work on the same project). Other relationships are variable (for example, Q must be assigned to either team 1 or team 3). Some relationships that are not stated explicitly in the conditions are implied by and can be deduced from those that are stated (for example, if one condition about paintings in a display specifies that Painting K must be to the left of Painting Y, and another specifies that Painting W must be to the left of Painting K, then it can be deduced that Painting W must be to the left of Painting Y).

In reading the conditions, do not introduce unwarranted assumptions. For instance, in a set of questions establishing relationships of height and weight among the members of a team, do not assume that a person who is taller than another person must weigh more than that person. As another example, suppose a set involves ordering and a question in the set asks what must be true if both X and Y must be earlier than Z; in this case, do not assume that X must be earlier than Y merely because X is mentioned before Y. All the information needed to answer each question is provided in the passage and the question itself.

The conditions are designed to be as clear as possible. Do not interpret the conditions as if they were intended to trick you. For example, if a question asks how many people could be eligible to serve on a committee, consider only those people named in the passage unless directed otherwise. When in doubt, read the conditions in their most obvious sense. Remember, however, that the language in the conditions is intended to be read for precise meaning. It is essential to pay particular attention to words that describe or limit relationships, such as "only," "exactly," "never," "always," "must be," "cannot be," and the like.

The result of this careful reading will be a clear picture of the structure of the relationships involved, including the kinds of relationships permitted, the participants in the relationships, and the range of possible actions or attributes for these participants.

Keep in mind question independence. Each question should be considered separately from the other questions in its set. No information, except what is given in the original conditions, should be carried over from one question to another.

In some cases a question will simply ask for conclusions to be drawn from the conditions as originally given. Some questions may, however, add information to the original conditions or temporarily suspend or replace one of the original conditions for the purpose of that question only. For example, if Question 1 adds the supposition "if P is sitting at table 2 ...," this supposition should NOT be carried over to any other question in the set.

Consider highlighting text and using diagrams. Many people find it useful to underline key points in the passage and in each question. In addition, it may prove very helpful to draw a diagram to assist you in finding the solution to the problem.

In preparing for the test, you may wish to experiment with different types of diagrams. For a scheduling problem, a simple calendar-like diagram may be helpful. For a grouping problem, an array of labeled columns or rows may be useful.

Even though most people find diagrams to be very helpful, some people seldom use them, and for some individual questions no one will need a diagram. There is by no means universal agreement on which kind of diagram is best for which problem or in which cases a diagram is most useful. Do not be concerned if a particular problem in the test seems to be best approached without the use of a diagram.

Logical Reasoning Questions

Arguments are a fundamental part of the law, and analyzing arguments is a key element of legal analysis. Training in the law builds on a foundation of basic reasoning skills. Law students must draw on the skills of analyzing, evaluating, constructing, and refuting arguments. They need to be able to identify what information is relevant to an issue or argument and what impact further evidence might have. They need to be able to reconcile opposing positions and use arguments to persuade others.

Logical Reasoning questions evaluate the ability to analyze, critically evaluate, and complete arguments as they occur in ordinary language. The questions are based on short arguments drawn from a wide variety of sources, including newspapers, general interest magazines, scholarly publications, advertisements, and informal discourse. These arguments mirror legal reasoning in the types of arguments presented and in their complexity, though few of the arguments actually have law as a subject matter.

Each Logical Reasoning question requires you to read and comprehend a short passage, then answer one question (or, rarely, two questions) about it. The questions are designed to assess a wide range of skills involved in thinking critically, with an emphasis on skills that are central to legal reasoning.

These skills include:

- Recognizing the parts of an argument and their relationships

- Recognizing similarities and differences between patterns of reasoning

- Drawing well-supported conclusions

- Reasoning by analogy

- Recognizing misunderstandings or points of disagreement

- Determining how additional evidence affects an argument

- Detecting assumptions made by particular arguments

- Identifying and applying principles or rules

- Identifying flaws in arguments

- Identifying explanations

The questions do not presuppose specialized knowledge of logical terminology. For example, you will not be expected to know the meaning of specialized terms such as "ad hominem" or "syllogism." On the other hand, you will be expected to understand and critique the reasoning contained in arguments. This requires that you possess a university-level understanding of widely used concepts such as argument, premise, assumption, and conclusion.

Suggested Approach
Read each question carefully. Make sure that you understand the meaning of each part of the question. Make sure that you understand the meaning of each answer choice and the ways in which it may or may not relate to the question posed.

Do not pick a response simply because it is a true statement. Although true, it may not answer the question posed.

Answer each question on the basis of the information that is given, even if you do not agree with it. Work within the context provided by the passage. LSAT questions do not involve any tricks or hidden meanings.

Reading Comprehension Questions

Both law school and the practice of law revolve around extensive reading of highly varied, dense, argumentative, and expository texts (for example, cases, codes, contracts, briefs, decisions, evidence). This reading must be exacting, distinguishing precisely what is said from what is not said. It involves comparison, analysis, synthesis, and application (for example, of principles and rules). It involves drawing appropriate inferences and applying ideas and arguments to new contexts. Law school reading also requires the ability to grasp unfamiliar subject matter and the ability to penetrate difficult and challenging material.

The purpose of LSAT Reading Comprehension questions is to measure the ability to read, with understanding and insight, examples of lengthy and complex materials similar to those commonly encountered in law school. The Reading Comprehension section of the LSAT contains four sets of reading questions, each set consisting of a selection of reading material followed by five to eight questions. The reading selection in three of the four sets consists of a single reading passage; the other set contains two related shorter passages. Sets with two passages are a variant of Reading Comprehension called Comparative Reading, which was introduced in June 2007.

Comparative Reading questions concern the relationships between the two passages, such as those of generalization/instance, principle/application, or point/counterpoint. Law school work often requires reading two or more texts in conjunction with each other and understanding their relationships. For example, a law student may read a trial court decision together with an appellate court decision that overturns it, or identify the fact pattern from a hypothetical suit together with the potentially controlling case law.

Reading selections for LSAT Reading Comprehension questions are drawn from a wide range of subjects in the humanities, the social sciences, the biological and physical sciences, and areas related to the law. Generally, the selections are densely written, use high-level vocabulary, and contain sophisticated argument or complex rhetorical structure (for example, multiple points of view). Reading Comprehension questions require you to read carefully and accurately, to determine the relationships among the various parts of the reading selection, and to draw reasonable inferences from the material in the selection. The questions may ask about the following characteristics of a passage or pair of passages:

- The main idea or primary purpose

- Information that is explicitly stated

- Information or ideas that can be inferred

- The meaning or purpose of words or phrases as used in context

- The organization or structure

- The application of information in the selection to a new context

- Principles that function in the selection

- Analogies to claims or arguments in the selection

- An author's attitude as revealed in the tone of a passage or the language used

- The impact of new information on claims or arguments in the selection

Suggested Approach

Since reading selections are drawn from many different disciplines and sources, you should not be discouraged if you encounter material with which you are not familiar. It is important to remember that questions are to be answered exclusively on the basis of the information provided in the selection. There is no particular knowledge that you are expected to bring to the test, and you should not make inferences based on any prior knowledge of a subject that you may have. You may, however, wish to defer working on a set of questions that seems particularly difficult or unfamiliar until after you have dealt with sets you find easier.

Strategies. One question that often arises in connection with Reading Comprehension has to do with the most effective and efficient order in which to read the selections and questions. Possible approaches include:

- reading the selection very closely and then answering the questions;

- reading the questions first, reading the selection closely, and then returning to the questions; or

- skimming the selection and questions very quickly, then rereading the selection closely and answering the questions.

Test takers are different, and the best strategy for one might not be the best strategy for another. In preparing for the test, therefore, you might want to experiment with the different strategies and decide what works most effectively for you.

Remember that your strategy must be effective under timed conditions. For this reason, the first strategy—reading the selection very closely and then answering the questions—may be the most effective for you. Nonetheless, if you believe that one of the other strategies

might be more effective for you, you should try it out and assess your performance using it.

Reading the selection. Whatever strategy you choose, you should give the passage or pair of passages at least one careful reading before answering the questions. Try to distinguish main ideas from supporting ideas, and opinions or attitudes from factual, objective information. Note transitions from one idea to the next and identify the relationships among the different ideas or parts of a passage, or between the two passages in Comparative Reading sets. Consider how and why an author makes points and draws conclusions. Be sensitive to implications of what the passages say.

You may find it helpful to mark key parts of passages. For example, you might underline main ideas or important arguments, and you might circle transitional words—"although," "nevertheless," "correspondingly," and the like—that will help you map the structure of a passage. Also, you might note descriptive words that will help you identify an author's attitude toward a particular idea or person.

Answering the Questions

- Always read all the answer choices before selecting the best answer. The best answer choice is the one that most accurately and completely answers the question being posed.

- Respond to the specific question being asked. Do not pick an answer choice simply because it is a true statement. For example, picking a true statement might yield an incorrect answer to a question in which you are asked to identify an author's position on an issue, since you are not being asked to evaluate the truth of the author's position but only to correctly identify what that position is.

- Answer the questions only on the basis of the information provided in the selection. Your own views, interpretations, or opinions, and those you have heard from others, may sometimes conflict with those expressed in a reading selection; however, you are expected to work within the context provided by the reading selection. You should not expect to agree with everything you encounter in Reading Comprehension passages.

THE WRITING SAMPLE

On the day of the test, you will be asked to write one sample essay. LSAC does not score the writing sample, but copies are sent to all law schools to which you apply. According to a 2006 LSAC survey of 157 United States and Canadian law schools, almost all use the writing sample in evaluating at least some applications for admission. Failure to respond to writing sample prompts and frivolous responses have been used by law schools as grounds for rejection of applications for admission.

In developing and implementing the writing sample portion of the LSAT, LSAC has operated on the following premises: First, law schools and the legal profession value highly the ability to communicate effectively in writing. Second, it is important to encourage potential law students to develop effective writing skills. Third, a sample of an applicant's writing, produced under controlled conditions, is a potentially useful indication of that person's writing ability. Fourth, the writing sample can serve as an independent check on other writing submitted by applicants as part of the admission process. Finally, writing samples may be useful for diagnostic purposes related to improving a candidate's writing.

The writing prompt presents a decision problem. You are asked to make a choice between two positions or courses of action. Both of the choices are defensible, and you are given criteria and facts on which to base your decision. There is no "right" or "wrong" position to take on the topic, so the quality of each test taker's response is a function not of which choice is made, but of how well or poorly the choice is supported and how well or poorly the other choice is criticized.

The LSAT writing prompt was designed and validated by legal education professionals. Since it involves writing based on fact sets and criteria, the writing sample gives applicants the opportunity to demonstrate the type of argumentative writing that is required in law school, although the topics are usually nonlegal.

You will have 35 minutes in which to plan and write an essay on the topic you receive. Read the topic and the accompanying directions carefully. You will probably find it best to spend a few minutes considering the topic and organizing your thoughts before you begin writing. In your essay, be sure to develop your ideas fully, leaving time, if possible, to review what you have written. Do not write on a topic other than the one specified. Writing on a topic of your own choice is not acceptable.

No special knowledge is required or expected for this writing exercise. Law schools are interested in the reasoning, clarity, organization, language usage, and writing mechanics displayed in your essay. How well you write is more important than how much you write. Confine your essay to the blocked, lined area on the front and back of the separate Writing Sample Response Sheet. Only that area will be reproduced for law schools. Be sure that your writing is legible.

TAKING THE PREPTEST UNDER SIMULATED LSAT CONDITIONS

One important way to prepare for the LSAT is to simulate the day of the test by taking a practice test under actual time constraints. Taking a practice test under timed conditions helps you to estimate the amount of time you can afford to spend on each question in a section and to determine the question types on which you may need additional practice.

Since the LSAT is a timed test, it is important to use your allotted time wisely. During the test, you may work only on the section designated by the test supervisor. You cannot devote extra time to a difficult section and make up that time on a section you find easier. In pacing yourself, and checking your answers, you should think of each section of the test as a separate minitest.

Be sure that you answer every question on the test. When you do not know the correct answer to a question, first eliminate the responses that you know are incorrect, then make your best guess among the remaining choices. Do not be afraid to guess as there is no penalty for incorrect answers.

When you take a practice test, abide by all the requirements specified in the directions and keep strictly within the specified time limits. Work without a rest period. When you take an actual test, you will have only a short break—usually 10–15 minutes—after SECTION III.

When taken under conditions as much like actual testing conditions as possible, a practice test provides very useful preparation for taking the LSAT.

Official directions for the four multiple-choice sections and the writing sample are included in this PrepTest so that you can approximate actual testing conditions as you practice.

To take the test:

- Set a timer for 35 minutes. Answer all the questions in SECTION I of this PrepTest. Stop working on that section when the 35 minutes have elapsed.

- Repeat, allowing yourself 35 minutes each for sections II, III, and IV.

- Set the timer again for 35 minutes, then prepare your response to the writing sample topic at the end of this PrepTest.

- Refer to "Computing Your Score" for the PrepTest for instruction on evaluating your performance. An answer key is provided for that purpose.

The practice test that follows consists of four sections corresponding to the four scored sections of the June 2013 LSAT. Also reprinted is the June 2013 unscored writing sample topic.

General Directions for the LSAT Answer Sheet

The actual testing time for this portion of the test will be 2 hours 55 minutes. There are five sections, each with a time limit of 35 minutes. The supervisor will tell you when to begin and end each section. If you finish a section before time is called, you may check your work on that section **only;** do not turn to any other section of the test book and do not work on any other section either in the test book or on the answer sheet.

There are several different types of questions on the test, and each question type has its own directions. **Be sure you understand the directions for each question type before attempting to answer any questions in that section.**

Not everyone will finish all the questions in the time allowed. Do not hurry, but work steadily and as quickly as you can without sacrificing accuracy. You are advised to use your time effectively. If a question seems too difficult, go on to the next one and return to the difficult question after completing the section. **MARK THE BEST ANSWER YOU CAN FOR EVERY QUESTION. NO DEDUCTIONS WILL BE MADE FOR WRONG ANSWERS. YOUR SCORE WILL BE BASED ONLY ON THE NUMBER OF QUESTIONS YOU ANSWER CORRECTLY.**

ALL YOUR ANSWERS MUST BE MARKED ON THE ANSWER SHEET. Answer spaces for each question are lettered to correspond with the letters of the potential answers to each question in the test book. After you have decided which of the answers is correct, blacken the corresponding space on the answer sheet. **BE SURE THAT EACH MARK IS BLACK AND COMPLETELY FILLS THE ANSWER SPACE.** Give only one answer to each question. If you change an answer, be sure that all previous marks are **erased completely.** Since the answer sheet is machine scored, incomplete erasures may be interpreted as intended answers. **ANSWERS RECORDED IN THE TEST BOOK WILL NOT BE SCORED.**

There may be more question numbers on this answer sheet than there are questions in a section. Do not be concerned, but be certain that the section and number of the question you are answering matches the answer sheet section and question number. Additional answer spaces in any answer sheet section should be left blank. Begin your next section in the number one answer space for that section.

LSAC takes various steps to ensure that answer sheets are returned from test centers in a timely manner for processing. In the unlikely event that an answer sheet is not received, LSAC will permit the examinee either to retest at no additional fee or to receive a refund of his or her LSAT fee. **THESE REMEDIES ARE THE ONLY REMEDIES AVAILABLE IN THE UNLIKELY EVENT THAT AN ANSWER SHEET IS NOT RECEIVED BY LSAC.**

Score Cancellation

Complete this section only if you are absolutely certain you want to cancel your score. **A CANCELLATION REQUEST CANNOT BE RESCINDED. IF YOU ARE AT ALL UNCERTAIN, YOU SHOULD NOT COMPLETE THIS SECTION.**

To cancel your score from this administration, you **must:**

A. fill in both ovals here ...... ○ ○
          AND
B. read the following statement. Then sign your name and enter the date. **YOUR SIGNATURE ALONE IS NOT SUFFICIENT FOR SCORE CANCELLATION. BOTH OVALS ABOVE MUST BE FILLED IN FOR SCANNING EQUIPMENT TO RECOGNIZE YOUR REQUEST FOR SCORE CANCELLATION.**

I certify that I wish to cancel my test score from this administration. I understand that my request is irreversible and that my score will not be sent to me or to the law schools to which I apply.

_____
Sign your name in full

_____
Date

FOR LSAC USE ONLY ⬤

HOW DID YOU PREPARE FOR THE LSAT?
(Select all that apply.)

Responses to this item are voluntary and will be used for statistical research purposes only.

○ By studying the free sample questions available on LSAC's website.
○ By taking the free sample LSAT available on LSAC's website.
○ By working through official LSAT *PrepTests*, *ItemWise*, and/or other LSAC test prep products.
○ By using LSAT prep books or software **not** published by LSAC.
○ By attending a commercial test preparation or coaching course.
○ By attending a test preparation or coaching course offered through an undergraduate institution.
○ Self study.
○ Other preparation.
○ No preparation.

CERTIFYING STATEMENT

Please write the following statement. Sign and date.

I certify that I am the examinee whose name appears on this answer sheet and that I am here to take the LSAT for the sole purpose of being considered for admission to law school. I further certify that I will neither assist nor receive assistance from any other candidate, and I agree not to copy, retain, or transmit examination questions in any form or discuss them with any other person.

_____
_____
_____
_____
_____
_____
_____
_____
_____

SIGNATURE: _____ TODAY'S DATE: ___/___/___
                                                           MONTH DAY YEAR

SCANTRON® EliteView™ EM-290725-3:654321

INSTRUCTIONS FOR COMPLETING THE BIOGRAPHICAL AREA ARE ON THE BACK COVER OF YOUR TEST BOOKLET.
USE ONLY A NO. 2 OR HB PENCIL TO COMPLETE THIS ANSWER SHEET. DO NOT USE INK.

A

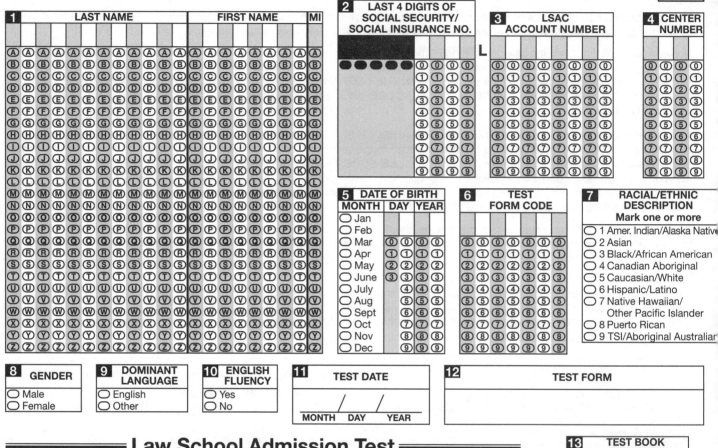

1 LAST NAME | FIRST NAME | MI

2 LAST 4 DIGITS OF SOCIAL SECURITY/ SOCIAL INSURANCE NO.

3 LSAC ACCOUNT NUMBER

4 CENTER NUMBER

5 DATE OF BIRTH
MONTH | DAY | YEAR
Jan, Feb, Mar, Apr, May, June, July, Aug, Sept, Oct, Nov, Dec

6 TEST FORM CODE

7 RACIAL/ETHNIC DESCRIPTION
Mark one or more
○ 1 Amer. Indian/Alaska Native
○ 2 Asian
○ 3 Black/African American
○ 4 Canadian Aboriginal
○ 5 Caucasian/White
○ 6 Hispanic/Latino
○ 7 Native Hawaiian/ Other Pacific Islander
○ 8 Puerto Rican
○ 9 TSI/Aboriginal Australian

8 GENDER
○ Male
○ Female

9 DOMINANT LANGUAGE
○ English
○ Other

10 ENGLISH FLUENCY
○ Yes
○ No

11 TEST DATE
MONTH DAY YEAR

12 TEST FORM

Law School Admission Test

Mark one and only one answer to each question. Be sure to fill in completely the space for your intended answer choice. If you erase, do so completely. Make no stray marks.

13 TEST BOOK SERIAL NO.

SECTION 1	SECTION 2	SECTION 3	SECTION 4	SECTION 5
1 Ⓐ Ⓑ Ⓒ Ⓓ Ⓔ	1 Ⓐ Ⓑ Ⓒ Ⓓ Ⓔ	1 Ⓐ Ⓑ Ⓒ Ⓓ Ⓔ	1 Ⓐ Ⓑ Ⓒ Ⓓ Ⓔ	1 Ⓐ Ⓑ Ⓒ Ⓓ Ⓔ
2 Ⓐ Ⓑ Ⓒ Ⓓ Ⓔ	2 Ⓐ Ⓑ Ⓒ Ⓓ Ⓔ	2 Ⓐ Ⓑ Ⓒ Ⓓ Ⓔ	2 Ⓐ Ⓑ Ⓒ Ⓓ Ⓔ	2 Ⓐ Ⓑ Ⓒ Ⓓ Ⓔ
3 Ⓐ Ⓑ Ⓒ Ⓓ Ⓔ	3 Ⓐ Ⓑ Ⓒ Ⓓ Ⓔ	3 Ⓐ Ⓑ Ⓒ Ⓓ Ⓔ	3 Ⓐ Ⓑ Ⓒ Ⓓ Ⓔ	3 Ⓐ Ⓑ Ⓒ Ⓓ Ⓔ
4 Ⓐ Ⓑ Ⓒ Ⓓ Ⓔ	4 Ⓐ Ⓑ Ⓒ Ⓓ Ⓔ	4 Ⓐ Ⓑ Ⓒ Ⓓ Ⓔ	4 Ⓐ Ⓑ Ⓒ Ⓓ Ⓔ	4 Ⓐ Ⓑ Ⓒ Ⓓ Ⓔ
5 Ⓐ Ⓑ Ⓒ Ⓓ Ⓔ	5 Ⓐ Ⓑ Ⓒ Ⓓ Ⓔ	5 Ⓐ Ⓑ Ⓒ Ⓓ Ⓔ	5 Ⓐ Ⓑ Ⓒ Ⓓ Ⓔ	5 Ⓐ Ⓑ Ⓒ Ⓓ Ⓔ
6 Ⓐ Ⓑ Ⓒ Ⓓ Ⓔ	6 Ⓐ Ⓑ Ⓒ Ⓓ Ⓔ	6 Ⓐ Ⓑ Ⓒ Ⓓ Ⓔ	6 Ⓐ Ⓑ Ⓒ Ⓓ Ⓔ	6 Ⓐ Ⓑ Ⓒ Ⓓ Ⓔ
7 Ⓐ Ⓑ Ⓒ Ⓓ Ⓔ	7 Ⓐ Ⓑ Ⓒ Ⓓ Ⓔ	7 Ⓐ Ⓑ Ⓒ Ⓓ Ⓔ	7 Ⓐ Ⓑ Ⓒ Ⓓ Ⓔ	7 Ⓐ Ⓑ Ⓒ Ⓓ Ⓔ
8 Ⓐ Ⓑ Ⓒ Ⓓ Ⓔ	8 Ⓐ Ⓑ Ⓒ Ⓓ Ⓔ	8 Ⓐ Ⓑ Ⓒ Ⓓ Ⓔ	8 Ⓐ Ⓑ Ⓒ Ⓓ Ⓔ	8 Ⓐ Ⓑ Ⓒ Ⓓ Ⓔ
9 Ⓐ Ⓑ Ⓒ Ⓓ Ⓔ	9 Ⓐ Ⓑ Ⓒ Ⓓ Ⓔ	9 Ⓐ Ⓑ Ⓒ Ⓓ Ⓔ	9 Ⓐ Ⓑ Ⓒ Ⓓ Ⓔ	9 Ⓐ Ⓑ Ⓒ Ⓓ Ⓔ
10 Ⓐ Ⓑ Ⓒ Ⓓ Ⓔ	10 Ⓐ Ⓑ Ⓒ Ⓓ Ⓔ	10 Ⓐ Ⓑ Ⓒ Ⓓ Ⓔ	10 Ⓐ Ⓑ Ⓒ Ⓓ Ⓔ	10 Ⓐ Ⓑ Ⓒ Ⓓ Ⓔ
11 Ⓐ Ⓑ Ⓒ Ⓓ Ⓔ	11 Ⓐ Ⓑ Ⓒ Ⓓ Ⓔ	11 Ⓐ Ⓑ Ⓒ Ⓓ Ⓔ	11 Ⓐ Ⓑ Ⓒ Ⓓ Ⓔ	11 Ⓐ Ⓑ Ⓒ Ⓓ Ⓔ
12 Ⓐ Ⓑ Ⓒ Ⓓ Ⓔ	12 Ⓐ Ⓑ Ⓒ Ⓓ Ⓔ	12 Ⓐ Ⓑ Ⓒ Ⓓ Ⓔ	12 Ⓐ Ⓑ Ⓒ Ⓓ Ⓔ	12 Ⓐ Ⓑ Ⓒ Ⓓ Ⓔ
13 Ⓐ Ⓑ Ⓒ Ⓓ Ⓔ	13 Ⓐ Ⓑ Ⓒ Ⓓ Ⓔ	13 Ⓐ Ⓑ Ⓒ Ⓓ Ⓔ	13 Ⓐ Ⓑ Ⓒ Ⓓ Ⓔ	13 Ⓐ Ⓑ Ⓒ Ⓓ Ⓔ
14 Ⓐ Ⓑ Ⓒ Ⓓ Ⓔ	14 Ⓐ Ⓑ Ⓒ Ⓓ Ⓔ	14 Ⓐ Ⓑ Ⓒ Ⓓ Ⓔ	14 Ⓐ Ⓑ Ⓒ Ⓓ Ⓔ	14 Ⓐ Ⓑ Ⓒ Ⓓ Ⓔ
15 Ⓐ Ⓑ Ⓒ Ⓓ Ⓔ	15 Ⓐ Ⓑ Ⓒ Ⓓ Ⓔ	15 Ⓐ Ⓑ Ⓒ Ⓓ Ⓔ	15 Ⓐ Ⓑ Ⓒ Ⓓ Ⓔ	15 Ⓐ Ⓑ Ⓒ Ⓓ Ⓔ
16 Ⓐ Ⓑ Ⓒ Ⓓ Ⓔ	16 Ⓐ Ⓑ Ⓒ Ⓓ Ⓔ	16 Ⓐ Ⓑ Ⓒ Ⓓ Ⓔ	16 Ⓐ Ⓑ Ⓒ Ⓓ Ⓔ	16 Ⓐ Ⓑ Ⓒ Ⓓ Ⓔ
17 Ⓐ Ⓑ Ⓒ Ⓓ Ⓔ	17 Ⓐ Ⓑ Ⓒ Ⓓ Ⓔ	17 Ⓐ Ⓑ Ⓒ Ⓓ Ⓔ	17 Ⓐ Ⓑ Ⓒ Ⓓ Ⓔ	17 Ⓐ Ⓑ Ⓒ Ⓓ Ⓔ
18 Ⓐ Ⓑ Ⓒ Ⓓ Ⓔ	18 Ⓐ Ⓑ Ⓒ Ⓓ Ⓔ	18 Ⓐ Ⓑ Ⓒ Ⓓ Ⓔ	18 Ⓐ Ⓑ Ⓒ Ⓓ Ⓔ	18 Ⓐ Ⓑ Ⓒ Ⓓ Ⓔ
19 Ⓐ Ⓑ Ⓒ Ⓓ Ⓔ	19 Ⓐ Ⓑ Ⓒ Ⓓ Ⓔ	19 Ⓐ Ⓑ Ⓒ Ⓓ Ⓔ	19 Ⓐ Ⓑ Ⓒ Ⓓ Ⓔ	19 Ⓐ Ⓑ Ⓒ Ⓓ Ⓔ
20 Ⓐ Ⓑ Ⓒ Ⓓ Ⓔ	20 Ⓐ Ⓑ Ⓒ Ⓓ Ⓔ	20 Ⓐ Ⓑ Ⓒ Ⓓ Ⓔ	20 Ⓐ Ⓑ Ⓒ Ⓓ Ⓔ	20 Ⓐ Ⓑ Ⓒ Ⓓ Ⓔ
21 Ⓐ Ⓑ Ⓒ Ⓓ Ⓔ	21 Ⓐ Ⓑ Ⓒ Ⓓ Ⓔ	21 Ⓐ Ⓑ Ⓒ Ⓓ Ⓔ	21 Ⓐ Ⓑ Ⓒ Ⓓ Ⓔ	21 Ⓐ Ⓑ Ⓒ Ⓓ Ⓔ
22 Ⓐ Ⓑ Ⓒ Ⓓ Ⓔ	22 Ⓐ Ⓑ Ⓒ Ⓓ Ⓔ	22 Ⓐ Ⓑ Ⓒ Ⓓ Ⓔ	22 Ⓐ Ⓑ Ⓒ Ⓓ Ⓔ	22 Ⓐ Ⓑ Ⓒ Ⓓ Ⓔ
23 Ⓐ Ⓑ Ⓒ Ⓓ Ⓔ	23 Ⓐ Ⓑ Ⓒ Ⓓ Ⓔ	23 Ⓐ Ⓑ Ⓒ Ⓓ Ⓔ	23 Ⓐ Ⓑ Ⓒ Ⓓ Ⓔ	23 Ⓐ Ⓑ Ⓒ Ⓓ Ⓔ
24 Ⓐ Ⓑ Ⓒ Ⓓ Ⓔ	24 Ⓐ Ⓑ Ⓒ Ⓓ Ⓔ	24 Ⓐ Ⓑ Ⓒ Ⓓ Ⓔ	24 Ⓐ Ⓑ Ⓒ Ⓓ Ⓔ	24 Ⓐ Ⓑ Ⓒ Ⓓ Ⓔ
25 Ⓐ Ⓑ Ⓒ Ⓓ Ⓔ	25 Ⓐ Ⓑ Ⓒ Ⓓ Ⓔ	25 Ⓐ Ⓑ Ⓒ Ⓓ Ⓔ	25 Ⓐ Ⓑ Ⓒ Ⓓ Ⓔ	25 Ⓐ Ⓑ Ⓒ Ⓓ Ⓔ
26 Ⓐ Ⓑ Ⓒ Ⓓ Ⓔ	26 Ⓐ Ⓑ Ⓒ Ⓓ Ⓔ	26 Ⓐ Ⓑ Ⓒ Ⓓ Ⓔ	26 Ⓐ Ⓑ Ⓒ Ⓓ Ⓔ	26 Ⓐ Ⓑ Ⓒ Ⓓ Ⓔ
27 Ⓐ Ⓑ Ⓒ Ⓓ Ⓔ	27 Ⓐ Ⓑ Ⓒ Ⓓ Ⓔ	27 Ⓐ Ⓑ Ⓒ Ⓓ Ⓔ	27 Ⓐ Ⓑ Ⓒ Ⓓ Ⓔ	27 Ⓐ Ⓑ Ⓒ Ⓓ Ⓔ
28 Ⓐ Ⓑ Ⓒ Ⓓ Ⓔ	28 Ⓐ Ⓑ Ⓒ Ⓓ Ⓔ	28 Ⓐ Ⓑ Ⓒ Ⓓ Ⓔ	28 Ⓐ Ⓑ Ⓒ Ⓓ Ⓔ	28 Ⓐ Ⓑ Ⓒ Ⓓ Ⓔ
29 Ⓐ Ⓑ Ⓒ Ⓓ Ⓔ	29 Ⓐ Ⓑ Ⓒ Ⓓ Ⓔ	29 Ⓐ Ⓑ Ⓒ Ⓓ Ⓔ	29 Ⓐ Ⓑ Ⓒ Ⓓ Ⓔ	29 Ⓐ Ⓑ Ⓒ Ⓓ Ⓔ
30 Ⓐ Ⓑ Ⓒ Ⓓ Ⓔ	30 Ⓐ Ⓑ Ⓒ Ⓓ Ⓔ	30 Ⓐ Ⓑ Ⓒ Ⓓ Ⓔ	30 Ⓐ Ⓑ Ⓒ Ⓓ Ⓔ	30 Ⓐ Ⓑ Ⓒ Ⓓ Ⓔ

14 PLEASE PRINT INFORMATION

LAST NAME

FIRST NAME

DATE OF BIRTH

● Ⓑ

THE PREPTEST

- Logical Reasoning ....SECTION I

- Analytical Reasoning..SECTION II

- Reading Comprehension...............................SECTION III

- Logical Reasoning ....SECTION IV

- Writing Sample Materials

SECTION I

Time—35 minutes

25 Questions

Directions: The questions in this section are based on the reasoning contained in brief statements or passages. For some questions, more than one of the choices could conceivably answer the question. However, you are to choose the best answer; that is, the response that most accurately and completely answers the question. You should not make assumptions that are by commonsense standards implausible, superfluous, or incompatible with the passage. After you have chosen the best answer, blacken the corresponding space on your answer sheet.

1. Police chief: This department's officers are, of course, prohibited from drinking on the job. However, there is one exception: it is extremely valuable for officers to work undercover to investigate nightclubs that have chronic crime problems, and officers may drink in moderation during such work.

Which one of the following, if true, most helps to justify the exception to the police department's rule stated above?

(A) Only very experienced police officers are allowed to work undercover investigating nightclubs.

(B) Many nightclub patrons would suspect that people in a nightclub who refrained from drinking were police officers.

(C) Over the last several years, the police department has significantly increased its undercover operations in nightclubs.

(D) Most police officers believe that allowing officers to drink during undercover work in nightclubs does not cause significant problems.

(E) For the most part, the public is aware that police officers are allowed to drink during undercover operations in nightclubs.

2. Jake: Companies have recently introduced antibacterial household cleaning products that kill common bacteria on surfaces like countertops and floors. It's clear that people who want to minimize the amount of bacteria in their homes should use cleaning products that contain antibacterial agents.

Karolinka: But studies also suggest that the use of these antibacterial cleaning products can be harmful, since common bacteria that survive the use of these products will eventually produce strains of bacteria that are resistant to antibiotics. That's why antibacterial agents should not be used in household cleaning products.

The discussion above indicates that Jake and Karolinka agree with each other that which one of the following is true?

(A) Household cleaning products with antibacterial agents kill some common bacteria.

(B) Household cleaning products with antibacterial agents remove dirt better than do products lacking those agents.

(C) The use of antibacterial agents in household cleaning products can produce antibiotic-resistant strains of bacteria.

(D) Common household bacteria are a serious health concern.

(E) People should use household cleaning products with antibacterial agents to clean their homes.

GO ON TO THE NEXT PAGE.

3. A study of the dietary habits of a group of people who had recently developed cancer and a group without cancer found that during the previous five years the diets of the two groups' members closely matched each other in the amount of yogurt they contained. Yogurt contains galactose, which is processed in the body by an enzyme. In the people with cancer the levels of this enzyme were too low to process the galactose in the yogurt they were consuming. It can be concluded that galactose in amounts exceeding the body's ability to process it is carcinogenic.

Of the following, which one constitutes the strongest objection to the reasoning in the argument?

(A)   The argument fails to consider whether the dietary habits of everyone in the two groups were the same in all other respects.
(B)   The argument neglects to recommend that people with low levels of the enzyme avoid eating yogurt.
(C)   The argument focuses on only one substance that can increase the risk of cancer, when it is well known that there are many such substances.
(D)   The argument overlooks the possibility that cancer causes low levels of the enzyme.
(E)   The argument does not specify whether any member of either group lacked the enzyme entirely.

4. Chemical-company employee: A conservation group's study of the pollutants released into the environment by 30 small chemical companies reveals that our company and four other companies together account for 60 percent of the total. Clearly, our company releases more pollutants than most chemical companies similar to us in size.

Which one of the following is an assumption required by the employee's argument?

(A)   The conservation group that produced the study is not hostile to the chemical industry.
(B)   The employee's company does not produce chemicals whose processing naturally produces more pollutants than the chemicals produced by other small chemical companies.
(C)   The total pollution produced by all small chemical companies combined is not greatly outweighed by that produced by large chemical companies.
(D)   The four other companies mentioned by the employee do not together account for very close to 60 percent of the total pollution by the 30 companies.
(E)   There is no significant variation in the quantities of pollutants released by the other 25 small chemical companies.

5. Journalist: A recent study showed that people who drink three cups of decaffeinated coffee per day are twice as likely to develop arthritis—inflammation of joints resulting from damage to connective tissue—as those who drink three cups of regular coffee per day. Clearly, decaffeinated coffee must contain something that damages connective tissue and that is not present in regular coffee.

Which one of the following would be most useful to know in order to evaluate the journalist's argument?

(A)   whether people who exercise regularly are more likely to drink decaffeinated beverages than those who do not
(B)   whether people who drink decaffeinated coffee tend to drink coffee less often than those who drink regular coffee
(C)   whether the degeneration of connective tissue is slowed by consumption of caffeine and other stimulants
(D)   whether most coffee drinkers drink more than three cups of coffee per day
(E)   whether people who have arthritis are less likely than the general population to drink coffee of any kind

6. A company that imports and sells collectibles sought to have some of its collectible figurines classified as toys, which are subject to lower import tariffs than collectibles. The company argued that the figurines amuse customers, just as toys do. However, the government agency responsible for tariffs rejected the company's request on the grounds that the figurines are marketed as collector's items rather than toys.

Which one of the following principles, if valid, most helps to justify the government agency's decision?

(A)   The tariff classification of an item should depend primarily on how the item is marketed.
(B)   When importing products, a company should seek the tariff classification that results in the lowest tariffs.
(C)   An object should not be classified as a collectible if it is typically used as a toy.
(D)   Objects that are developed primarily to provide amusement should be subject to lower tariffs than other objects.
(E)   A company should market its products as collectibles rather than toys if doing so enables it to sell them for higher prices.

GO ON TO THE NEXT PAGE.

7. The photographs that the store developed were quite unsatisfactory. The customer claims to have handled the film correctly. Neither the film nor the camera was defective. If a store does not process pictures properly, the customer is owed a refund, so if the customer's claim is correct, the store owes her a refund.

The argument relies on assuming which one of the following?

(A) If the store owes the customer a refund, then neither the camera nor the film was defective.

(B) If neither the film nor the camera was defective, and the customer handled the film correctly, then the store processed it improperly.

(C) If pictures are taken with a defective camera, then it is not possible for the store to develop those pictures improperly.

(D) If the customer handled the film incorrectly, that is what caused the photographs that the store developed to be unsatisfactory.

(E) If the customer's claim was not correct, then the store does not owe her a refund.

8. When weeding a vegetable garden, one should not try to remove all the weeds. It is true that the more weeds, the less productive the garden. Nevertheless, avoiding the painstaking effort of finding and pulling every single weed more than compensates for the slight productivity loss resulting from leaving a few.

The principle underlying which one of the following arguments is most similar to the principle underlying the argument above?

(A) It is a mistake to try to remove every imperfection from one's personality. Personality imperfections make life difficult sometimes, but people cannot be truly happy if their personalities lack defects.

(B) One should not try to change every aspect of one's personality. Such a radical change is more likely to make one worse off than better off.

(C) If one is trying to improve one's personality by removing imperfections, one should not try to remove them all. For while each imperfection makes one's personality worse, it is no longer worth one's time to remove imperfections if there are only a few left.

(D) One who is trying to improve one's personality by removing imperfections should not try to remove them all. Granted, the fewer imperfections one's personality has, the happier one will be. However, it is never possible to remove all of the imperfections from one's personality.

(E) When one is trying to improve one's personality, one should not try to remove imperfections that do not cause one serious difficulties. Often, removing such an imperfection will only lead to greater imperfections.

GO ON TO THE NEXT PAGE.

9. Doctor: It would benefit public health if junk food were taxed. Not only in this country but in many other countries as well, the excessive proportion of junk food in people's diets contributes to many common and serious health problems. If junk food were much more expensive than healthful food, people would be encouraged to make dietary changes that would reduce these problems.

Which one of the following most accurately expresses the conclusion drawn in the doctor's argument?

(A)   Taxing junk food would benefit public health.
(B)   In many countries, the excessive proportion of junk food in people's diets contributes to many common and serious health problems.
(C)   If junk food were much more expensive than healthful food, people would be encouraged to make dietary changes that would reduce many common and serious health problems.
(D)   Taxing junk food would encourage people to reduce the proportion of junk food in their diets.
(E)   Junk food should be taxed if doing so would benefit public health.

10. Large deposits of the rare mineral nahcolite formed in salty lakes 50 million to 52 million years ago during the Eocene epoch. Laboratory tests found that, in salty water, nahcolite can form only when the atmosphere contains at least 1,125 parts per million of carbon dioxide.

The statements above, if true, most strongly support which one of the following?

(A)   For most of the time since the Eocene epoch, the level of carbon dioxide in the atmosphere has been lower than it was during most of the Eocene epoch.
(B)   Levels of carbon dioxide in the atmosphere fluctuated greatly during the Eocene epoch.
(C)   Lakes were more likely to be salty during periods when the level of carbon dioxide in the atmosphere was at least 1,125 parts per million.
(D)   The atmosphere contained at least 1,125 parts per million of carbon dioxide during at least some part of the Eocene epoch.
(E)   No significant deposits of nahcolite have formed at any time since the Eocene epoch.

11. Editor: When asked to name a poet contemporaneous with Shakespeare, 60 percent of high school students picked a twentieth-century poet. Admittedly, it is hard to interpret this result accurately. Does it show that most high school students do not know any poets of Shakespeare's era, or do they just not know what "contemporaneous" means? However, either way, there is clearly something deeply wrong with the educational system.

The statement that the majority of students picked a twentieth-century poet functions primarily in the argument

(A)   as evidence that the educational system is producing students who are ignorant of the history of poetry
(B)   as evidence of the ambiguity of some questions
(C)   to illustrate that research results are difficult to interpret
(D)   as evidence that the ambiguity of data should not prevent us from drawing conclusions from them
(E)   as evidence that something is deeply wrong with the educational system

12. One should apologize only to a person one has wronged, and only for having wronged that person. To apologize sincerely is to acknowledge that one has acted wrongfully. One cannot apologize sincerely unless one intends not to repeat that wrongful act. To accept an apology sincerely is to acknowledge a wrong, but also to vow not to hold a grudge against the wrongdoer.

The statements above, if true, most strongly support which one of the following?

(A)   If one apologizes and subsequently repeats the wrongful act for which one has apologized, then one has not apologized sincerely.
(B)   One cannot sincerely accept an apology that was not sincerely offered.
(C)   If one commits a wrongful act, then one should sincerely apologize for that act.
(D)   An apology that cannot be sincerely accepted cannot be sincerely offered.
(E)   An apology cannot be both sincerely offered and sincerely accepted unless each person acknowledges that a wrongful act has occurred.

GO ON TO THE NEXT PAGE.

13. A small collection of copper-alloy kitchen implements was found in an abandoned Roman-era well. Beneath them was a cache of coins, some of which dated to 375 A.D. The implements, therefore, were dropped into the well no earlier than 375 A.D.

Which one of the following, if true, most strengthens the argument?

(A) The coins used in the Roman Empire often remained in circulation for many decades.
(B) The coins were found in a dense cluster that could not have been formed by coins slipping through an accumulation of larger objects.
(C) The coins had far more value than the kitchen implements did.
(D) The items in the well were probably thrown there when people evacuated the area and would have been retrieved if the people had returned.
(E) Items of jewelry found beneath the coins were probably made around 300 A.D.

14. Investigators have not proved that the forest fire was started by campers. Nor have they proved that lightning triggered the fire. So the investigators have not proved that the blaze was caused by campers or lightning.

The flawed pattern of reasoning in which one of the following arguments most closely resembles the flawed pattern of reasoning in the argument above?

(A) Kim has no reason to believe that Sada will win the election. Kim also has no reason to believe that Brown will win the election. So Kim has no reason to believe that either Sada or Brown will win the election.
(B) We have no proof either for the theory that the thief escaped through the vent in the ceiling or for the theory that the thief escaped through the window. Therefore, one theory is as plausible as the other.
(C) Most of the students in my dormitory are engineering majors, and most of the students in my dormitory are from out of town. So most of the engineering majors in my dormitory are from out of town.
(D) In some parts of the forest camping is permitted. Also, hunting is permitted in some parts of the forest. So there are some parts of the forest in which both hunting and camping are permitted.
(E) The evidence shows that the car could have been driven by Jones at the time of the accident; however, it also shows that it could have been driven by Katsarakis at the time of the accident. Therefore, the evidence shows that the car could have been driven by both Jones and Katsarakis at the time of the accident.

15. To reduce the mosquito population in a resort area, hundreds of trees were planted that bear fruit attractive to birds. Over the years, as the trees matured, they attracted a variety of bird species and greatly increased the summer bird population in the area. As expected, the birds ate many mosquitoes. However, the planting of the fruit trees had the very opposite of its intended effect.

Which one of the following, if true, most helps to explain the apparently paradoxical result?

(A) Most of the species of birds that were attracted by the trees that were planted did not eat mosquitoes.
(B) The species of birds that were attracted in the greatest number by the fruit of the trees that were planted did not eat mosquitoes.
(C) The birds attracted to the area by the trees ate many more insects that prey on mosquitoes than they did mosquitoes.
(D) Since the trees were planted, the annual precipitation has been below average, and drier weather tends to keep mosquito populations down.
(E) Increases and decreases in mosquito populations tend to follow a cyclical pattern.

16. Roxanne promised Luke that she would finish their report while he was on vacation; however, the deadline for that report was postponed. Clearly, if you promised a friend that you would meet them for lunch but just before lunch you felt ill, it would not be wrong for you to miss the lunch; your friend would not expect you to be there if you felt ill. Similarly, _____.

Which one of the following most logically completes the argument?

(A) if Roxanne believes that Luke would not expect her to finish the report under the circumstances, then it would be wrong for Roxanne to finish it
(B) it would not be wrong for Roxanne to finish the report if Luke did not expect the deadline to be postponed
(C) if Luke would expect Roxanne to finish the report even after the deadline has been postponed, then it would be wrong for Roxanne not to finish it
(D) if Luke would not expect Roxanne to finish the report under the circumstances, then it would not be wrong for Roxanne to fail to finish it
(E) Luke would not expect Roxanne to finish the report and it would be wrong if she did finish it

GO ON TO THE NEXT PAGE.

17.   Politician: A major social problem is children hurting other children. The results of a recent experiment by psychologists establish that watching violent films is at least partly responsible for this aggressive behavior. The psychologists conducted an experiment in which one group of children watched a film of people punching Bobo the Clown dolls. A second group of children was not shown the film. Afterward, both groups of children played together in a room containing a Bobo doll. Most of the children who had seen the film punched the Bobo doll, while most of the other children did not.

Which one of the following, if true, most weakens the politician's argument?

(A)   Some of the children who did not punch the Bobo doll, including some who had been shown the film, chastised those who did punch the doll.

(B)   The child who punched the Bobo doll the hardest and the most frequently had not been shown the film.

(C)   The children who had been shown the film were found to be no more likely than the children who had not been shown the film to punch other children.

(D)   Some children who had not been shown the film imitated the behavior of those who had been shown the film and who punched the doll.

(E)   Many of the children who participated in the experiment had never seen a Bobo doll before the experiment.

18.   Editorial: In order to encourage personal responsibility in adults, society should not restrict the performance of any of the actions of adults or interfere with the likely results except to prevent negative effects on others.

Which one of the following expresses a view that is inconsistent with the principle stated in the editorial?

(A)   We should not prevent the students from wasting the classroom time set aside for homework. But this does not mean that they may spend the time any way they wish. Activities disruptive to others should not be tolerated.

(B)   The scientist who invented this technology is not the only one who should be allowed to profit from it. After all, there is no evidence that allowing others to profit from this technology will reduce the scientist's own profits.

(C)   Even though public smoking may lead to indirect harm to others, it should not be banned. There are several other ways to eliminate this harm that do not restrict the conduct of smokers and hence are preferable to a complete ban on public smoking.

(D)   Highway speed limits are a justified restriction of freedom. For drivers who speed do not risk only their own lives; such drivers often injure or kill other people. Moreover, speed limits have been shown to significantly reduce highway accident and fatality rates.

(E)   It is not enough that consumable products containing harmful substances have warning labels. Many adults simply ignore such warnings and continue to consume these substances in spite of the harm it may cause them. This is why consuming such substances should be illegal.

GO ON TO THE NEXT PAGE.

19. The goblin fern, which requires a thick layer of leaf litter on the forest floor, is disappearing from North American forests. In spots where it has recently vanished, the leaf litter is unusually thin and, unlike those places where this fern still thrives, is teeming with the European earthworm *Lumbricus rubellus*, which eats leaf litter. *L. rubellus* is thus probably responsible for the fern's disappearance.

Which one of the following is an assumption on which the argument depends?

(A) Wherever there is a thick layer of leaf litter in North American forests, goblin ferns can be found.

(B) None of the earthworms that are native to North America eat leaf litter.

(C) Dead leaves from goblin ferns make up the greater part of the layer of leaf litter on the forest floors where the goblin fern has recently vanished.

(D) There are no spots in the forests of North America where both goblin ferns and earthworms of the species *L. rubellus* can be found.

(E) *L. rubellus* does not favor habitats where the leaf litter layer is considerably thinner than what is required by goblin ferns.

20. Medical reporter: Studies have consistently found that taking an aspirin a day thins the blood slightly, thereby helping to prevent or reduce the severity of heart disease. Since heart disease is one of the most common types of ill health in industrialized nations, most people in such nations would therefore be in better health if they took an aspirin a day.

The reasoning in the doctor's argument is most vulnerable to criticism on which one of the following grounds?

(A) It takes for granted that if medication can reduce the severity of heart disease, it can also prevent some cases of heart disease.

(B) It overlooks the possibility that even if a disease is one of the most common in a nation, most people in that nation are not in significant danger of developing that disease.

(C) It overlooks the possibility that preventing or reducing the severity of heart disease has little or no effect on any of the other most common diseases in industrialized nations.

(D) It fails to address the possibility that taking an aspirin a day is not the single most effective measure for preventing heart disease.

(E) It fails to address the possibility that the studies on the beneficial effects of aspirin were conducted only in industrialized nations.

21. Essayist: Winners of a Nobel prize for science, who are typically professional scientists, have all made significant contributions to science. But amateur scientists have also provided many significant contributions. And unlike professional scientists, who are often motivated by economic necessity or a desire for fame, amateur scientists are motivated by the love of discovery alone.

If the essayist's statements are true, then which one of the following must also be true?

(A) Some amateur scientists who did not win a Nobel prize for science nevertheless made significant contributions to science.

(B) Typically, winners of a Nobel prize for science are not motivated at all by the love of discovery.

(C) The love of discovery is the motive behind many significant contributions to science.

(D) Professional scientists have made a greater overall contribution to science than have amateur scientists.

(E) A professional scientist is more likely to make a significant contribution to science if he or she is motivated by the love of discovery.

22. Company president: Most of our best sales representatives came to the job with a degree in engineering but little or no sales experience. Thus, when we hire sales representatives, we should favor applicants who have engineering degrees but little or no sales experience over applicants with extensive sales experience but no engineering degrees.

Which one of the following, if true, most seriously weakens the company president's argument?

(A) Some of the company's sales representatives completed a degree in engineering while working for the company.

(B) Most of the people hired by the company as sales representatives have had a degree in engineering but no sales experience.

(C) Most of the customers that the company's sales representatives work with have a degree in engineering.

(D) Most of the people who apply for a sales representative position with the company do not have a degree in engineering.

(E) Some of the people who the company has hired as sales representatives and who were subsequently not very good at the job did not have extensive previous sales experience.

GO ON TO THE NEXT PAGE.

23. Anthropologist: Every human culture has taboos against eating certain animals. Some researchers have argued that such taboos originated solely for practical reasons, pointing out, for example, that in many cultures it is taboo to eat domestic animals that provide labor and that are therefore worth more alive than dead. But that conclusion is unwarranted; taboos against eating certain animals might instead have arisen for symbolic, ritualistic reasons, and the presence of the taboos might then have led people to find other uses for those animals.

In the argument, the anthropologist

(A) calls an explanation of a phenomenon into question by pointing out that observations cited as evidence supporting it are also compatible with an alternative explanation of the phenomenon

(B) establishes that an explanation of a phenomenon is false by demonstrating that the evidence that had been cited in support of that explanation was inadequate

(C) rejects the reasoning used to justify a hypothesis about the origins of a phenomenon, on the grounds that there exists another, more plausible hypothesis about the origins of that phenomenon

(D) argues in support of one explanation of a phenomenon by citing evidence incompatible with a rival explanation

(E) describes a hypothesis about the sequence of events involved in the origins of a phenomenon, and then argues that those events occurred in a different sequence

24. In an effort to reduce underage drinking, the Department of Health has been encouraging adolescents to take a pledge not to drink alcohol until they reach the legal age. This seems to be successful. A survey of seventeen-year-olds has found that many who do not drink report having taken a pledge to refrain from drinking, whereas almost all who drink report having never taken such a pledge.

The reasoning in the argument is most vulnerable to criticism because the argument

(A) bases a conclusion about the efficacy of a method to reduce underage drinking merely on a normative judgment about the morality of underage drinking

(B) fails to consider that an alternative method of reducing underage drinking might be more effective

(C) infers from an association between pledging not to drink and refraining from drinking that the pledging was the cause of refraining from drinking

(D) treats a condition that is sufficient to produce an outcome as though it were necessary for the outcome to occur

(E) confuses the claim that many adolescents who do not drink report having taken the pledge with the claim that many who report having taken the pledge do not drink

25. Literary critic: A folktale is a traditional story told in an entertaining way, which may lead some to think that folktales lack deeper meaning. But this is not the case. A folktale is passed along by a culture for generations, and each storyteller adds something of his or her own to the story, and in this way folktales provide great insight into the wisdom of the culture.

The main conclusion of the literary critic's argument can be properly inferred if which one of the following is assumed?

(A) Any tale that is passed along by a culture for generations can provide great insight into the wisdom of that culture.

(B) Any tale that provides insight into the wisdom of a culture is deeply meaningful in some respect.

(C) Not every tale that lacks deep meaning or beauty is told solely for entertainment.

(D) Any tale with deep meaning provides great insight into the wisdom of the culture by which it has been passed on.

(E) A story that is told primarily for entertainment does not necessarily lack deeper meaning.

S T O P

IF YOU FINISH BEFORE TIME IS CALLED, YOU MAY CHECK YOUR WORK ON THIS SECTION ONLY.
DO NOT WORK ON ANY OTHER SECTION IN THE TEST.

SECTION II

Time—35 minutes

23 Questions

Directions: Each group of questions in this section is based on a set of conditions. In answering some of the questions, it may be useful to draw a rough diagram. Choose the response that most accurately and completely answers each question and blacken the corresponding space on your answer sheet.

Questions 1–5

A researcher is studying seven manuscripts—F, G, H, L, M, P, and S—to determine their relative ages. It is known that no two manuscripts were written at the same time. The researcher has also determined the following:

H was written earlier than S but later than F.
P was the next manuscript written after G.
At least four of the manuscripts were written earlier than L.
At least four of the manuscripts were written later than M.
H was not written fifth.

1. Which one of the following could be the order in which the manuscripts were written, from first to last?

(A)   F, M, G, H, P, L, S
(B)   G, P, M, F, H, S, L
(C)   H, F, M, G, P, L, S
(D)   L, F, M, G, P, H, S
(E)   M, F, H, S, L, G, P

GO ON TO THE NEXT PAGE.

2. Which one of the following manuscripts CANNOT have been written third?

(A) S
(B) P
(C) M
(D) H
(E) G

3. If H was the next manuscript written after M, which one of the following could be true?

(A) F was written second.
(B) G was written third.
(C) H was written fourth.
(D) P was written third.
(E) S was written fourth.

4. Which one of the following manuscripts CANNOT have been written fourth?

(A) F
(B) G
(C) H
(D) P
(E) S

5. If P was written earlier than H, then any of the following could be true EXCEPT:

(A) F was written first.
(B) G was written third.
(C) H was written sixth.
(D) L was written seventh.
(E) M was written second.

GO ON TO THE NEXT PAGE.

Questions 6–11

Exactly six petri dishes—labeled dish 1 through dish 6—are to be stored in an otherwise empty refrigerator. There are three available shelves—the bottom shelf, the middle shelf, and the top shelf. The placement of the dishes must be consistent with the following conditions:

No more than three dishes are stored on any shelf.
Dish 2 is stored at least one shelf above dish 6.
Dish 6 is stored either one shelf above or one shelf below dish 5.
Dish 1 is not stored on the same shelf as dish 4.

6. Which one of the following is an acceptable placement of dishes on the bottom, middle, and top shelves?

(A)   bottom: dish 1
        middle: dish 6
        top: dishes 2, 3, 4, 5
(B)   bottom: dishes 1, 3
        middle: dish 6
        top: dishes 2, 4, 5
(C)   bottom: dish 2
        middle: dishes 4, 6
        top: dishes 1, 3, 5
(D)   bottom: dishes 3, 5
        middle: dish 6
        top: dishes 1, 2, 4
(E)   bottom: dishes 4, 6
        middle: dishes 1, 3
        top: dishes 2, 5

GO ON TO THE NEXT PAGE.

7. If dish 6 is the only dish stored on the bottom shelf, which one of the following could be the list of dishes that are stored together on the middle shelf?

   (A) dish 1, dish 3
   (B) dish 2, dish 4
   (C) dish 2, dish 3
   (D) dish 3, dish 5
   (E) dish 4, dish 5

8. If dish 1, dish 2, and dish 3 are stored on the same shelf as each other, which one of the following could be true?

   (A) Exactly one of the dishes is stored on the top shelf.
   (B) Exactly two of the dishes are stored on the top shelf.
   (C) Exactly two of the dishes are stored on the middle shelf.
   (D) Exactly three of the dishes are stored on the middle shelf.
   (E) Exactly three of the dishes are stored on the bottom shelf.

9. If exactly one of the shelves has no dish stored on it, which one of the following must be true?

   (A) Exactly three of the dishes are stored on the bottom shelf.
   (B) Exactly three of the dishes are stored on the middle shelf.
   (C) Dish 1 is stored on the same shelf as dish 5.
   (D) Dish 2 is stored on the same shelf as dish 3.
   (E) Dish 4 is stored on the same shelf as dish 5.

10. If dish 5 is the only dish stored on the bottom shelf and if exactly two of the dishes are stored on the middle shelf, then which one of the following is a pair of dishes that must be among the dishes stored on the top shelf?

    (A) dish 1 and dish 2
    (B) dish 1 and dish 6
    (C) dish 2 and dish 3
    (D) dish 2 and dish 4
    (E) dish 3 and dish 4

11. If exactly one of the dishes is stored on the middle shelf, which one of the following could be the list of dishes stored on the top shelf?

    (A) dish 1, dish 2
    (B) dish 1, dish 5
    (C) dish 2, dish 3
    (D) dish 3, dish 4
    (E) dish 3, dish 5

GO ON TO THE NEXT PAGE.

Questions 12–17

A company operates vending machines in four schools: Ferndale, Gladstone, Hafford, and Isley. The company delivers juices in one of its two trucks and snacks in the other truck. Each week, exactly one delivery of juices and exactly one delivery of snacks is made to each school, subject to the following conditions:

Snacks must be delivered to Ferndale at some time before they are delivered to Hafford.

Gladstone cannot be the fourth school to which juices are delivered.

Gladstone must be the third school to which snacks are delivered.

The first school to which juices are delivered must be the fourth one to which snacks are delivered.

12. Which one of the following could be the schedule of deliveries to the schools, from the first to the fourth?

(A)   Juices: Hafford, Ferndale, Gladstone, Isley
        Snacks: Ferndale, Isley, Gladstone, Hafford

(B)   Juices: Hafford, Isley, Ferndale, Gladstone
        Snacks: Isley, Ferndale, Gladstone, Hafford

(C)   Juices: Isley, Ferndale, Gladstone, Hafford
        Snacks: Hafford, Ferndale, Gladstone, Isley

(D)   Juices: Isley, Gladstone, Ferndale, Hafford
        Snacks: Ferndale, Gladstone, Hafford, Isley

(E)   Juices: Isley, Hafford, Gladstone, Ferndale
        Snacks: Ferndale, Isley, Gladstone, Hafford

GO ON TO THE NEXT PAGE.

13. If Hafford is the fourth school to which juices are delivered, which one of the following must be true?

   (A) Ferndale is the second school to which juices are delivered.
   (B) Gladstone is the third school to which juices are delivered.
   (C) Ferndale is the second school to which snacks are delivered.
   (D) Hafford is the second school to which snacks are delivered.
   (E) Isley is the first school to which snacks are delivered.

14. If Isley is the third school to which juices are delivered, which one of the following could be true?

   (A) Juices are delivered to Gladstone at some time before they are delivered to Hafford.
   (B) Juices are delivered to Isley at some time before they are delivered to Hafford.
   (C) Snacks are delivered to Ferndale at some time before they are delivered to Isley.
   (D) Snacks are delivered to Gladstone at some time before they are delivered to Isley.
   (E) Snacks are delivered to Hafford at some time before they are delivered to Gladstone.

15. If Isley is the first school to which snacks are delivered, which one of the following could be true?

   (A) Ferndale is the second school to which juices are delivered.
   (B) Hafford is the second school to which juices are delivered.
   (C) Hafford is the third school to which juices are delivered.
   (D) Isley is the first school to which juices are delivered.
   (E) Hafford is the second school to which snacks are delivered.

16. Which one of the following could be true?

   (A) Both juices and snacks are delivered to Gladstone at some time before they are delivered to Ferndale.
   (B) Both juices and snacks are delivered to Gladstone at some time before they are delivered to Isley.
   (C) Both juices and snacks are delivered to Hafford at some time before they are delivered to Isley.
   (D) Both juices and snacks are delivered to Isley at some time before they are delivered to Ferndale.
   (E) Both juices and snacks are delivered to Isley at some time before they are delivered to Hafford.

17. Which one of the following, if substituted for the condition that Gladstone cannot be the fourth school to which juices are delivered, would have the same effect in determining the delivery schedule?

   (A) Ferndale must be either the second school or the fourth school to which juices are delivered.
   (B) Gladstone must be either the second school or the third school to which juices are delivered.
   (C) Hafford must be either the first school or the fourth school to which juices are delivered.
   (D) The first school to which juices are delivered must be either Ferndale or Isley.
   (E) The fourth school to which juices are delivered must be either Hafford or Isley.

GO ON TO THE NEXT PAGE.

Questions 18–23

Each of five paralegals—Frank, Gina, Hiro, Kevin, and Laurie—is being assigned to exactly one of three cases—the Raimes, Sicoli, or Thompson case. At least one paralegal will be assigned to each case. The following conditions must apply:

Either Frank is assigned to Raimes and Kevin is assigned to Thompson, or Frank is not assigned to Raimes and Kevin is not assigned to Thompson.

Either Frank is the sole paralegal assigned to his case or Gina is the sole paralegal assigned to her case, but not both.

Hiro is assigned to Sicoli.

18. Which one of the following could be the assignment of paralegals to cases?

(A) Raimes: Frank
     Sicoli: Gina, Hiro, Kevin
     Thompson: Laurie
(B) Raimes: Kevin
     Sicoli: Gina
     Thompson: Frank, Hiro, Laurie
(C) Raimes: Gina, Kevin
     Sicoli: Frank, Hiro
     Thompson: Laurie
(D) Raimes: Kevin, Laurie
     Sicoli: Gina, Hiro
     Thompson: Frank
(E) Raimes: Frank, Kevin, Laurie
     Sicoli: Hiro
     Thompson: Gina

GO ON TO THE NEXT PAGE.

19. Which one of the following CANNOT be the complete assignment of paralegals to the Sicoli case?

    (A) Frank, Hiro, Kevin
    (B) Frank, Hiro, Laurie
    (C) Gina, Hiro, Kevin
    (D) Gina, Hiro, Laurie
    (E) Hiro, Kevin, Laurie

20. If exactly two of the paralegals are assigned to the Thompson case, then which one of the following could be the complete assignment of paralegals to the Raimes case?

    (A) Gina
    (B) Kevin
    (C) Laurie
    (D) Gina, Kevin
    (E) Kevin, Laurie

21. If one of the cases has Gina and Laurie as the only paralegals assigned to it, then each of the following must be false EXCEPT:

    (A) Frank is assigned to the Raimes case.
    (B) Frank is assigned to the Sicoli case.
    (C) Gina is assigned to the Raimes case.
    (D) Kevin is assigned to the Raimes case.
    (E) Laurie is assigned to the Thompson case.

22. Which one of the following CANNOT be the complete assignment of paralegals to the Thompson case?

    (A) Gina
    (B) Laurie
    (C) Gina, Kevin
    (D) Gina, Laurie
    (E) Kevin, Laurie

23. If Kevin is the sole paralegal assigned to one of the cases, then which one of the following lists all of the paralegals any one of whom could be assigned to the Raimes case?

    (A) Frank, Kevin, Laurie
    (B) Frank, Kevin
    (C) Frank
    (D) Gina
    (E) Kevin

S T O P

IF YOU FINISH BEFORE TIME IS CALLED, YOU MAY CHECK YOUR WORK ON THIS SECTION ONLY.
DO NOT WORK ON ANY OTHER SECTION IN THE TEST.

SECTION III
Time—35 minutes
27 Questions

<u>Directions</u>: Each set of questions in this section is based on a single passage or a pair of passages. The questions are to be answered on the basis of what is <u>stated</u> or <u>implied</u> in the passage or pair of passages. For some of the questions, more than one of the choices could conceivably answer the question. However, you are to choose the <u>best</u> answer; that is, the response that most accurately and completely answers the question, and blacken the corresponding space on your answer sheet.

The prevailing trend in agriculture toward massive and highly mechanized production, with its heavy dependence on debt and credit as a means of raising capital, has been linked to the growing problem
(5) of bankruptcy among small farms. African American horticulturalist Booker T. Whatley has proposed a comprehensive approach to small farming that runs counter to this trend. Whatley maintains that small farms can operate profitably despite these economic
(10) obstacles, and he provides guidelines that he believes will bring about such profitability when combined with smart management and hard work.

Whatley emphasizes that small farms must generate year-round cash flow. To this end, he
(15) recommends growing at least ten different crops, which would alleviate financial problems should one crop fail completely. To minimize the need to seek hard-to-obtain loans, the market for the farm products should be developed via a "clientele membership club"
(20) (CMC), whereby clients pay in advance for the right to go to the farm and harvest what they require. To help guarantee small farmers a market for all of their crops, Whatley encourages them to grow only crops that clients ask for, and to comply with client requests
(25) regarding the use of chemicals.

Whatley stresses that this "pick-your-own" farming is crucial for profitability because 50 percent of a farmer's production cost is tied up with harvesting, and using clients as harvesters allows the farmer to
(30) charge 60 percent of what supermarkets charge and still operate the farm at a profit. Whatley's plan also affords farmers the advantage of selling directly to consumers, thus eliminating distribution costs. To realize profits on a 25-acre farm, for example,
(35) Whatley suggests that a CMC of about 1,000 people is needed. The CMC would consist primarily of people from metropolitan areas who value fresh produce.

The success of this plan, Whatley cautions, depends in large part on a farm's location: the farm
(40) should be situated on a hard-surfaced road within 40 miles of a population center of at least 50,000 people, as studies suggest that people are less inclined to travel any greater distances for food. In this way, Whatley reverses the traditional view of hard-surfaced
(45) roads as farm-to-market roads, calling them instead "city-to-farm" roads. The farm should also have well-drained soil and a ready water source for irrigation, since inevitably certain preferred crops will not be drought resistant. Lastly, Whatley recommends
(50) carrying liability insurance upwards of $1 million to

cover anyone injured on the farm. Adhering to this plan, Whatley contends, will allow small farms to exist as a viable alternative to sprawling corporate farms while providing top-quality agricultural goods
(55) to consumers in most urban areas.

1. Which one of the following most accurately states the main point of the passage?

(A) In reaction to dominant trends in agriculture, Booker T. Whatley has advanced a set of recommendations he claims will enable small farms to thrive.

(B) Booker T. Whatley's approach to farming is sensitive to the demands of the consumer, unlike the dominant approach to farming that focuses on massive and efficient production and depends on debt and credit.

(C) As part of a general critique of the trend in agriculture toward massive production, Booker T. Whatley assesses the ability of small farms to compete against large corporate farms.

(D) While CMCs are not the only key to successful small farming, Booker T. Whatley shows that without them small farms risk failure even with a diversity of crops and a good location.

(E) The adoption of Booker T. Whatley's methods of small farming will eventually threaten the dominance of large-scale production and reliance on debt and credit that mark corporate farming.

GO ON TO THE NEXT PAGE.

2. Based on the information in the passage, which one of the following would Whatley be most likely to view as facilitating adherence to an aspect of his plan for operating a small farm?

    (A) a farmer's planting a relatively unknown crop to test the market for that crop

    (B) a farmer's leaving large lanes between plots of each crop to allow people easy access at harvest time

    (C) a farmer's traveling into the city two afternoons a week to sell fresh produce at a farmer's market

    (D) a farmer's using an honor system whereby produce is displayed on tables in view of the road and passersby can buy produce and leave their money in a box

    (E) a farmer's deciding that for environmental reasons chemicals will no longer be used on the farm to increase yields

3. According to the passage, "pick-your-own" farming is seen by Whatley as necessary to the operation of small farms for which one of the following reasons?

    (A) Customers are given the chance to experience firsthand where their produce comes from.

    (B) It guarantees a substantial year-round cash flow for the farm.

    (C) It allows farmers to maintain profits while charging less for produce than what supermarkets charge.

    (D) Only those varieties of crops that have been specifically selected by clients within the CMC will be grown by the farmer.

    (E) Consumers who are willing to drive to farms to harvest their own food comprise a strong potential market for farmers.

4. The author of the passage is primarily concerned with

    (A) summarizing the main points of an innovative solution to a serious problem

    (B) examining contemporary trends and isolating their strengths and weaknesses

    (C) criticizing widely accepted practices within a key sector of the economy

    (D) demonstrating the advantages and disadvantages of a new strategy within an industry

    (E) analyzing the impact of a new idea on a tradition-driven industry

5. The passage provides the most support for inferring which one of the following statements?

    (A) A corporate farm is more likely to need a loan than a small farm is.

    (B) If small farms charged what supermarkets charge for produce that is fresher than that sold by supermarkets, then small farms would see higher profits in the long term.

    (C) Consumers who live in rural areas are generally less inclined than those who live in metropolitan areas to join a CMC.

    (D) If a CMC requests fewer than ten different crops to be grown, then at least one of Whatley's recommendations will not be followed.

    (E) Distribution costs are accounted for in the budget of a small farm with a CMC and are paid directly by customers.

6. According to the passage, Whatley advocates which one of the following actions because it would help to guarantee that small farms have buyers for all of their produce?

    (A) growing at least ten different crops

    (B) charging 60 percent of what supermarkets charge for the same produce

    (C) recruiting only clients who value fresh produce

    (D) honoring the crop requests and chemical-use preferences of clients

    (E) irrigating crops that are susceptible to drought

7. Which one of the following inferences is most supported by the information in the passage?

    (A) The advance payment to the farmer by CMC members guarantees that members will get the produce they want.

    (B) Hard-surfaced roads are traditionally the means by which some farmers transport their produce to their customers in cities.

    (C) A typical population center of 50,000 should be able to support CMCs on at least fifty 25-acre farms.

    (D) Consumers prefer hard-surfaced roads to other roads because the former cause less wear and tear on their vehicles.

    (E) Most roads with hard surfaces were originally given these surfaces primarily for the sake of farmers.

GO ON TO THE NEXT PAGE.

When Jayne Hinds Bidaut saw her first tintype, she was so struck by its rich creamy tones that she could hardly believe this photographic process had been abandoned. She set out to revive it. Bidaut had
(5) been searching for a way to photograph insects from her entomological collection, but paper prints simply seemed too flat to her. The tintype, an image captured on a thin, coated piece of iron (there is no tin in it), provided the detail and dimensionality she wanted.
(10) The image-containing emulsion can often create a raised surface on the plate.

For the photographer Dan Estabrook, old albumen prints and tintypes inspired a fantasy. He imagines planting the ones he makes in flea markets and antique
(15) shops, to be discovered as "originals" from a bygone time that never existed.

On the verge of a filmless, digital revolution, photography is moving forward into its past. In addition to reviving the tintype process, photographers
(20) are polishing daguerreotype plates, coating paper with egg whites, making pinhole cameras, and mixing emulsions from nineteenth-century recipes in order to coax new expressive effects from old photographic techniques. So diverse are the artists returning to
(25) photography's roots that the movement is more like a groundswell.

The old techniques are heavily hands-on and idiosyncratic. That is the source of their appeal. It is also the prime reason for their eclipse. Most became
(30) obsolete in a few decades, replaced by others that were simpler, cheaper, faster, and more consistent in their results. Only the tintype lasted as a curiosity into the twentieth century. Today's artists quickly discover that to exploit the past is to court the very uncertainty that
(35) early innovators sought to banish. Such unpredictability attracted Estabrook to old processes. His work embraces accident and idiosyncrasy in order to foster the illusion of antiquity. In his view, time leaches meaning from every photograph and renders it a lost object, enabling
(40) us to project onto it our sentiments and associations. So while the stains and imperfections of prints made from gum bichromate or albumen coatings would probably have been cropped out by a nineteenth-century photographer, Estabrook retains them to
(45) heighten the sense of nostalgia.

This preoccupation with contingency offers a clue to the deeper motivations of many of the antiquarian avant-gardists. The widely variable outcome of old techniques virtually guarantees that
(50) each production is one of a kind and bears, on some level, the indelible mark of the artist's encounter with a particular set of circumstances. At the same time, old methods offer the possibility of recovering an intimacy with photographic communication that
(55) mass media have all but overwhelmed.

8. In the context of the third paragraph, the function of the phrase "on the verge of a filmless, digital revolution" (line 17) is to

(A) highlight the circumstances that make the renewed interest in early photographic processes ironic

(B) indicate that most photographers are wary of advanced photographic techniques

(C) reveal the author's skeptical views regarding the trend toward the use of old photographic techniques

(D) suggest that most photographers who are artists see little merit in the newest digital technology

(E) imply that the groundswell of interest by photographers in old processes will probably turn out to be a passing fad

9. Based on the passage, which one of the following most accurately describes an attitude displayed by the author toward artists' uses of old photographic techniques?

(A) doubtful hesitation about the artistic value of using old techniques

(B) appreciative understanding of the artists' aesthetic goals

(C) ironic amusement at the continued use of techniques that are obsolete

(D) enthusiastic endorsement of their implicit critique of modern photographic technology

(E) whimsical curiosity about the ways in which the processes work

10. Information in the passage most helps to answer which one of the following questions?

(A) What are some nineteenth-century photographic techniques that have not been revived?

(B) What is the chemical makeup of the emulsion applied to the iron plate in the tintype process?

(C) What are the names of some contemporary photographers who are using pinhole cameras?

(D) What effect is produced when photographic paper is coated with egg whites?

(E) What were the perceived advantages of the innovations that led to the obsolescence of many early photographic techniques and processes?

GO ON TO THE NEXT PAGE.

11. Which one of the following most accurately describes the primary purpose of the passage?

    (A) to make a case for the aesthetic value of certain old photographic processes
    (B) to provide details of how certain old methods of photographic processing are used in producing artistic photographs
    (C) to give an account of a surprising recent development in the photographic arts
    (D) to explain the acclaim that photographers using old photographic techniques have received
    (E) to contrast the approaches used by two contemporary photographers

12. Which one of the following is most analogous to the use of old photographic techniques for artistic purposes by late-twentieth-century artists, as described in the passage?

    (A) A biomedical researcher in a pharmaceutical firm researches the potential of certain traditional herbal remedies for curing various skin conditions.
    (B) An architect investigates ancient accounts of classical building styles in order to get inspiration for designing a high-rise office building.
    (C) An engineer uses an early-twentieth-century design for a highly efficient turbocharger in preference to a new computer-aided design.
    (D) A clothing designer uses fabrics woven on old-fashioned looms in order to produce the irregular texture of handwoven garments.
    (E) An artist uses a computer graphics program to reproduce stylized figures from ancient paintings and insert them into a depiction of a modern city landscape.

13. Based on the information in the passage, it can be inferred that Estabrook believes that

    (A) photography in the nineteenth century tended to focus on subjects that are especially striking and aesthetically interesting
    (B) artists can relinquish control over significant aspects of the process of creating their work and still produce the aesthetic effects they desire
    (C) photographs produced in the nineteenth and early twentieth centuries were generally intended to exploit artistically the unpredictability of photographic processing
    (D) it is ethically questionable to produce works of art intended to deceive the viewer into believing that the works are older than they really are
    (E) the aesthetic significance of a photograph depends primarily on factors that can be manipulated after the photograph has been taken

14. The reasoning by which, according to the passage, Estabrook justifies his choice of certain strategies in photographic processing would be most strengthened if which one of the following were true?

    (A) When advanced modern photographic techniques are used to intentionally produce prints with imperfections resembling those in nineteenth-century prints, the resulting prints invariably betray the artifice involved.
    (B) The various feelings evoked by a work of art are independent of the techniques used to produce the work and irrelevant to its artistic value.
    (C) Most people who use photographs as a way of remembering or learning about the past value them almost exclusively for their ability to record their subjects accurately.
    (D) People who are interested in artistic photography seldom see much artistic value in photographs that appear antique but are not really so.
    (E) The latest photographic techniques can produce photographs that are almost completely free of blemishes and highly resistant to deterioration over time.

GO ON TO THE NEXT PAGE.

Passage A is from a 2007 article on the United States patent system; passage B is from a corporate statement.

Passage A

Theoretically, the patent office is only supposed to award patents for "nonobvious" inventions, and the concept of translating between an Internet address and a telephone number certainly seems obvious. Still,

(5) a court recently held that a technology company had infringed on patents covering computer servers that perform these translations.

In an ideal world, patents would be narrow enough that companies could "invent around" others'

(10) patents if licensing agreements cannot be reached. Unfortunately, the patent system has departed from this ideal. In recent decades, the courts have dramatically lowered the bar for obviousness. As a result, some patents being granted are so broad that

(15) inventing around them is practically impossible.

Large technology companies have responded to this proliferation of bad patents with the patent equivalent of nuclear stockpiling. By obtaining hundreds or even thousands of patents, a company

(20) can develop a credible deterrent against patent lawsuits: if someone sues it for patent infringement, it can find a patent the other company has infringed and countersue. Often, however, a fundamental mistake is made: not joining this arms race. As a result, a

(25) company can find itself defenseless against lawsuits.

Software patents are particularly ripe for abuse because software is assembled from modular components. If the patent system allows those components to be patented, it becomes almost

(30) impossible to develop a software product without infringing numerous patents. Moreover, because of the complexity of software, it is often prohibitively expensive to even find all the patents a given software product might in principle be infringing. So even a

(35) software maker that wanted to find and license all of the patents relevant to its products is unlikely to be able to do so.

Passage B

Software makers like ours have consistently taken the position that patents generally impede innovation

(40) in software development and are inconsistent with open-source/free software. We will continue to work to promote this position and are pleased to join our colleagues in the open-source/free software community, as well as those proprietary vendors who have publicly

(45) stated their opposition to software patents.

At the same time, we are forced to live in the world as it is, and that world currently permits software patents. A small number of very large companies have amassed large numbers of software

(50) patents. We believe such massive software patent portfolios are ripe for misuse because of the questionable nature of many software patents generally and because of the high cost of patent litigation.

One defense against such misuse is to develop a

(55) corresponding portfolio of software patents for defensive purposes. Many software makers, both open-source and proprietary, pursue this strategy. In the interests of our company and in an attempt to protect and promote the open-source community,

(60) we have elected to adopt this same stance. We do so reluctantly because of the perceived inconsistency with our stance against software patents; however, prudence dictates this position.

15. Which one of the following pairs would be most appropriate as titles for passage A and passage B, respectively?

(A) "The Use and Abuse of Patents"
"The Necessary Elimination of Software Patents"
(B) "Reforming Patent Laws"
"In Defense of Software Patents"
(C) "Patenting the Obvious"
"Patents: A Defensive Policy"
(D) "A Misunderstanding of Patent Policies"
"Keeping Software Free but Safe"
(E) "Developing a Credible Deterrent Against Patent Lawsuits"
"An Apology to Our Customers"

16. Which one of the following is mentioned in passage A but not in passage B?

(A) the amassing of patents by software companies
(B) the cost of finding all the patents a product may infringe
(C) the negative effect of patents on software development
(D) the high cost of patent litigation in general
(E) the dubious nature of many software patents

17. Which one of the following comes closest to capturing the meaning of the phrase "invent around" (line 9)?

(A) invent a product whose use is so obvious that no one can have a patent on it
(B) conceal the fact that a product infringes a patent
(C) implement a previously patented idea in a way other than that intended by the patent holder
(D) develop new products based on principles that are entirely different from those for products affected by competitors' patents
(E) devise something that serves the same function as the patented invention without violating the patent

GO ON TO THE NEXT PAGE.

18. Which one of the following most accurately describes the relationship between the two passages?

   (A)   Passage A objectively reports a set of events; passage B subjectively takes issue with aspects of the reported events.
   (B)   Passage A discusses a problem in an industry; passage B states the position of a party dealing with that problem.
   (C)   Passage A is highly critical of a defensive strategy used by an industry; passage B is a clarification of that strategy.
   (D)   Passage A describes an impasse within an industry; passage B suggests a way out of this impasse.
   (E)   Passage A lays out both sides of a dispute; passage B focuses on one of those sides.

19. The authors of the passages would be most likely to agree that software companies would be well advised to

   (A)   amass their own portfolios of software patents
   (B)   attempt to license software patented by other companies
   (C)   exploit patents already owned by competitors
   (D)   refrain from infringing on any patents held by other companies
   (E)   research the patents relevant to their products more thoroughly

20. In terms of what it alludes to, "this same stance" (line 60) is most closely related to which one of the following phrases in passage A?

   (A)   nonobvious (line 2)
   (B)   invent around (line 9)
   (C)   lowered the bar (line 13)
   (D)   credible deterrent (line 20)
   (E)   modular components (lines 27–28)

21. Which one of the following, if true, would cast doubt on the position concerning innovation in software development taken in the first paragraph of passage B?

   (A)   Most patents for software innovations have a duration of only 20 years or less.
   (B)   Software companies that do not patent software generally offer products that are more reliable than those that do.
   (C)   Some proprietary vendors oppose software patents for self-interested reasons.
   (D)   Software innovation would be less profitable if software could not be patented.
   (E)   The main beneficiaries of software innovations are large corporations rather than individual innovators.

GO ON TO THE NEXT PAGE.

Calvaria major is a rare but once-abundant tree found on the island of Mauritius, which was also home to the dodo, a large flightless bird that became extinct about three centuries ago. In 1977 Stanley Temple,
(5) an ecologist whose investigation of *Calvaria major* was a sidelight to his research on endangered birds of Mauritius, proposed that the population decline of *Calvaria major* was linked to the demise of the dodo, a hypothesis that subsequently gained considerable
(10) currency. Temple had found only thirteen *Calvaria major* trees on Mauritius, all overmature and dying, and all estimated by foresters at over 300 years old. These trees produced fruits that appeared fertile but that Temple assumed could no longer germinate,
(15) given his failure to find younger trees.

The temporal coincidence between the extinction of the dodo and what Temple considered the last evidence of natural germination of *Calvaria major* seeds led him to posit a causal connection. Specifically,
(20) he hypothesized that the fruit of *Calvaria major* had developed its extremely thick-walled pit as an evolutionary response to the dodo's habitual consumption of those fruits, a trait enabling the pits to withstand the abrasive forces exerted on them in
(25) the birds' digestive tracts. This defensive thickness, though, ultimately prevented the seeds within the pits from germinating without the thinning caused by abrasion in the dodo's gizzard. What had once been adaptive, Temple maintained, became a lethal
(30) imprisonment for the seeds after the dodo vanished.

Although direct proof was unattainable, Temple did offer some additional findings in support of his hypothesis, which lent his argument a semblance of rigor. From studies of other birds, he estimated the
(35) abrasive force generated within a dodo's gizzard. Based on this estimate and on test results determining the crush-resistant strength of *Calvaria major* pits, he concluded that the pits could probably have withstood a cycle through a dodo's gizzard. He also fed *Calvaria*
(40) *major* pits to turkeys, and though many of the pits were destroyed, ten emerged, abraded yet intact. Three of these sprouted when planted, which he saw as vindicating his hypothesis.

Though many scientists found this dramatic and
(45) intriguing hypothesis plausible, Temple's proposals have been strongly challenged by leading specialists in the field. Where Temple had found only thirteen specimens of *Calvaria major*, Wendy Strahm, the foremost expert on the plant ecology of Mauritius,
(50) has identified hundreds, many far younger than three centuries. So *Calvaria major* seeds have in fact germinated, and the tree's reproductive cycle has thus continued, since the dodo's disappearance. Additional counterevidence comes from horticultural
(55) research by Anthony Speke, which shows that while only a minority of unabraded *Calvaria major* seeds germinate, the number is still probably sufficient to keep this species from becoming extinct. The population decline, while clearly acute, could easily
(60) be due to other factors, including disease and damage done by certain nonindigenous animals introduced onto Mauritius in the past few centuries.

22. Which one of the following most accurately expresses the main point of the passage?

(A) *Calvaria major* germination, though rare, is probably adequate to avoid extinction of the species.

(B) The appeal of Temple's hypothesis notwithstanding, the scarcity of *Calvaria major* is probably not due to the extinction of the dodo.

(C) Temple's experimentation with *Calvaria major* pits, though methodologically unsound, nevertheless led to a probable solution to the mystery of the tree's decline.

(D) Temple's dramatic but speculative hypothesis, though presented without sufficient supporting research, may nevertheless be correct.

(E) *Calvaria major* would probably still be scarce today even if the dodo had not become extinct.

23. The author indicates that Temple's research on birds of the island of Mauritius

(A) was largely concerned with species facing the threat of extinction

(B) furnished him with the basis for his highly accurate estimates of the crush-resistant strength of *Calvaria major* pits

(C) provided experimental evidence that some modern birds' gizzards exert roughly the same amount of abrasive force on their contents as did dodo gizzards

(D) was comprehensive in scope and conducted with methodological precision

(E) was originally inspired by his observation that apparently fertile *Calvaria major* pits were nevertheless no longer able to germinate

GO ON TO THE NEXT PAGE.

24. In saying that Temple's supporting evidence lent his argument a "semblance of rigor" (lines 33–34), the author most likely intends to indicate that

(A)   despite his attempts to use strict scientific methodology, Temple's experimental findings regarding *Calvaria major* pits were not carefully derived and thus merely appeared to support his hypothesis

(B)   direct proof of a hypothesis of the sort Temple was investigating is virtually impossible to obtain, even with the most exact measurements and observations

(C)   in contrast to Temple's secondhand information concerning the age of the thirteen overmature *Calvaria major* trees he found, his experiments with turkeys and other birds represented careful and accurate firsthand research

(D)   in his experimentation on *Calvaria major* pits, Temple produced quantitative experimental results that superficially appeared to bolster the scientific credibility of his hypothesis

(E)   although the consensus among experts is that Temple's overall conclusion is mistaken, the scientific precision and the creativity of Temple's experimentation remain admirable

25. The passage indicates which one of the following about the abrasion of *Calvaria major* pit walls?

(A)   Thinning through abrasion is not necessary for germination of *Calvaria major* seeds.

(B)   In Temple's experiment, the abrasion caused by the digestive tracts of turkeys always released *Calvaria major* seeds, undamaged, from their hard coverings.

(C)   Temple was mistaken in believing that the abrasion caused by dodos would have been sufficient to thin the pit walls to any significant degree.

(D)   Abrasion of *Calvaria major* pit walls by the digestive tracts of animals occurred commonly in past centuries but rarely occurs in nature today.

(E)   Temple overlooked the fact that other natural environmental forces have been abrading *Calvaria major* pit walls since the dodo ceased to fulfill this role.

26. It can be most logically inferred from the passage that the author regards Temple's hypothesis that the extinction of the dodo was the cause of *Calvaria major*'s seeming loss of the ability to reproduce as which one of the following?

(A)   essentially correct, but containing some inaccurate details

(B)   initially implausible, but vindicated by his empirical findings

(C)   an example of a valuable scientific achievement outside a researcher's primary area of expertise

(D)   laudable for its precise formulation and its attention to historical detail

(E)   an attempt to explain a state of affairs that did not in fact exist

27. Based on the passage, it can be inferred that the author would be likely to agree with each of the following statements about *Calvaria major* EXCEPT:

(A)   The causes of the evolution of the tree's particularly durable pit wall have not been definitively identified by Temple's critics.

(B)   The notion that the thickness of the pit wall in the tree's fruit has been a factor contributing to the decline of the tree has not been definitively discredited.

(C)   In light of the current rate of germination of seeds of the species, it is surprising that the tree has not been abundant since the dodo's disappearance.

(D)   There is good reason to believe that the tree is not threatened with imminent extinction.

(E)   *Calvaria major* seeds can germinate even if they do not first pass through a bird's digestive system.

S T O P

IF YOU FINISH BEFORE TIME IS CALLED, YOU MAY CHECK YOUR WORK ON THIS SECTION ONLY.
DO NOT WORK ON ANY OTHER SECTION IN THE TEST.

SECTION IV

Time—35 minutes

25 Questions

<u>Directions:</u> The questions in this section are based on the reasoning contained in brief statements or passages. For some questions, more than one of the choices could conceivably answer the question. However, you are to choose the <u>best</u> answer; that is, the response that most accurately and completely answers the question. You should not make assumptions that are by commonsense standards implausible, superfluous, or incompatible with the passage. After you have chosen the best answer, blacken the corresponding space on your answer sheet.

1. Scientists generally believe that no deep-sea creature can detect red light, but they need to reassess that view. Researchers recently discovered a foot-long deep-sea creature of the genus *Erenna* with bioluminescent red lights on some of its tentacles. These red lights, which are shaped like a common food source for small, deep-sea fish, probably function as lures to attract prey.

   Which one of the following most accurately expresses the overall conclusion drawn in the argument?

   (A) Red lights on the tentacles of a newly discovered deep-sea creature probably function as lures.
   (B) Red lights on the tentacles of a newly discovered deep-sea creature are shaped like a common food source for small, deep-sea fish.
   (C) A foot-long deep-sea creature of the genus *Erenna* has been discovered recently.
   (D) Scientists generally believe that deep-sea creatures cannot detect red light.
   (E) Scientists need to reconsider the belief that deep-sea creatures cannot detect red light.

2. For house painting, acrylic paints are an excellent choice. They provide everything that a good paint should provide: smooth and even coverage, quick drying time, durability, and easy cleanup. Even acrylics, however, cannot correct such surface defects as badly cracked paint. Such conditions indicate some underlying problem, such as water damage, that needs repair.

   Which one of the following is most strongly supported by the statements above?

   (A) Badly cracked paint is not a result of harsh weather conditions.
   (B) Acrylics are the only paints that provide everything that most homeowners need from a paint.
   (C) Acrylics should not be used to paint over other types of house paint.
   (D) It is not a requirement of house paints that they correct surface defects such as badly cracked paint.
   (E) Acrylic paints come in as wide a range of colors as do any other paints.

3. Letter to the editor: You have asserted that philanthropists want to make the nonprofit sector as efficient as private business in this country. Philanthropists want no such thing, of course. Why would anyone want to make nonprofits as inefficient as Byworks Corporation, which has posted huge losses for years?

   The reasoning of the argument in the letter is most vulnerable to criticism on the grounds that the argument

   (A) draws a conclusion about what ought to be the case from premises that are entirely about what is the case
   (B) takes the condition of one member of a category to be representative of the category in general
   (C) rejects a claim by attacking the proponent of the claim rather than addressing the claim itself
   (D) concludes that a claim must be false because of the mere absence of evidence in its favor
   (E) concludes that a phenomenon will have a certain property merely because the phenomenon's cause has that property

GO ON TO THE NEXT PAGE.

4.   Statistical records of crime rates probably often reflect as much about the motives and methods of those who compile or cite them as they do about the actual incidence of crime. The police may underreport crime in order to convey the impression of their own success or overreport crime to make the case for a budget increase. Politicians may magnify crime rates to get elected or minimize them to remain in office. Newspapers, of course, often sensationalize crime statistics to increase readership.

The argument proceeds by doing which one of the following?

(A)   evaluating evidence for and against its conclusion
(B)   citing examples in support of its conclusion
(C)   deriving implications of a generalization that it assumes to be true
(D)   enumerating problems for which it proposes a general solution
(E)   showing how evidence that apparently contradicts its conclusion actually supports that conclusion

5.   Physiologist: The likelihood of developing osteoporosis is greatly increased by a deficiency of calcium in the diet. Dairy products usually contain more calcium per serving than do fruits and vegetables. Yet in countries where dairy products are rare, and fruits and vegetables are the main source of calcium, the incidence of osteoporosis is much lower than in countries where people consume a great deal of calcium from dairy products.

Which one of the following, if true, would most help to resolve the apparent discrepancy described by the physiologist?

(A)   A healthy human body eventually loses the excess calcium that it takes in.
(B)   Many people who eat large quantities of fruits and vegetables also consume dairy products.
(C)   There are more people who have a calcium deficiency than there are who have developed osteoporosis.
(D)   People who have calcium deficiencies are also likely to have deficiencies in other minerals.
(E)   The fats in dairy products tend to inhibit the body's calcium absorption.

6.   A first-term board member should not be on the finance committee unless he or she is an accountant or his or her membership on the committee is supported by all the members of the board.

Which one of the following arguments most closely conforms to the principle stated above?

(A)   Simkins is a first-term board member and not an accountant; thus, Simkins should not be on the finance committee.
(B)   Timmons is a third-term board member but not an accountant; thus, if all other board members think that Timmons should be on the finance committee, then Timmons should be on that committee.
(C)   Ruiz is on the finance committee but is not an accountant; thus, Ruiz's membership must have been supported by all the members of the board.
(D)   Klein is a first-term board member who is not an accountant; thus, Klein should not be allowed on the finance committee if any board member opposes Klein's appointment to that committee.
(E)   Mabry is a board member who is not an accountant; thus, because Mabry's membership on the finance committee is opposed by most board members, Mabry should not be allowed on that committee.

7.   Most respondents to a magazine survey who had recently listened to a taped reading of a certain best-selling novel said that they had enjoyed the novel, while most respondents who had recently read the novel themselves said they had not enjoyed it. These survey results support the contention that a person who listens to a taped reading of a novel is more likely to enjoy the novel than a person who reads it is.

Which one of the following, if true, would most weaken the argument?

(A)   Most of the respondents who had listened to a taped reading of the novel had never read it, and most of the respondents who had read the novel had never listened to a taped reading of it.
(B)   Most people can read a novel in considerably less time than it would take them to listen to a taped reading of it.
(C)   When people are asked their opinion of a best-selling novel that they have read or listened to on tape, they are more likely to say that they enjoyed the novel than that they did not enjoy it.
(D)   Many novels that are available in text versions are not available in audio versions.
(E)   The novel in question, unlike most novels, included dialogue in many different dialects that are more understandable when heard than when read.

GO ON TO THE NEXT PAGE.

8. To qualify as a medical specialist, one must usually graduate from a university, then complete approximately four years of medical school, followed by a residency of two to six years in one's specialty. Finally, a physician who desires to become a recognized specialist must complete an evaluation program directed by a medical specialty board. Therefore, anyone who has qualified as a recognized medical specialist is competent to practice in his or her specialty.

Which one of the following is an assumption on which the argument depends?

(A)   People who are not highly motivated will not complete the demanding course of study and examination required to become qualified as a recognized medical specialist.

(B)   Only the most talented people will successfully complete the rigorous course of study necessary for qualification as a recognized medical specialist.

(C)   No one incompetent to practice a particular specialty completes the evaluation program for that specialty.

(D)   Usually, six to ten years of medical training beyond a university degree is sufficient to render someone competent to practice in his or her medical specialty.

(E)   Usually, six to ten years of medical training beyond a university degree is necessary to render someone competent to practice in his or her medical specialty.

9. Archaeologists are currently analyzing plant remains found at a site that was last occupied more than 10,000 years ago. If the plants were cultivated, then the people who occupied the site discovered agriculture thousands of years before any other people are known to have done so. On the other hand, if the plants were wild—that is, uncultivated—then the people who occupied the site ate a wider variety of wild plants than did any other people at the time.

The statements above, if true, most strongly support which one of the following?

(A)   The archaeologists analyzing the plant remains at the site will be able to determine whether the plants were cultivated or were wild.

(B)   The people who occupied the site used some plants in ways that no other people did at that time.

(C)   If the people who occupied the site had reached a more advanced stage in the use of wild plants than any other people at the time, then the plants found at the site were uncultivated.

(D)   If the people who occupied the site discovered agriculture thousands of years before people anywhere else are known to have done so, then there are remains of cultivated plants at the site.

(E)   It is more likely that the people who occupied the site discovered agriculture thousands of years before people anywhere else did than it is that they ate a wider variety of wild plants than any other people at the time.

GO ON TO THE NEXT PAGE.

10. In a test of fuel efficiency, car X and car Y yielded the same average fuel mileage, even though car X was driven in a less fuel-efficient manner than car Y was. Thus, car X is more fuel efficient than car Y.

Which one of the following arguments is most similar in its reasoning to the argument above?

(A) In an experiment, subject X consistently gave lower pain ratings in response to pinpricks than subject Y did. Therefore, it is reasonable to conclude that subjects X and Y experience pain differently.

(B) Our hamster gained the same amount of weight as our neighbors' hamster, even though our hamster ate more than theirs. So it must be that our hamster burned more calories than theirs did.

(C) When on his bicycle, Roland makes better time coasting down a hill than pedaling on a horizontal path. So he would make even better time on the hills if he were to pedal rather than coast.

(D) When asked to judge the value of various pieces of antique furniture, I gave lower estimates on average than you did. So in those cases where we both gave the same estimate, I must have overestimated the piece's value.

(E) Jean demonstrates a high level of visual acuity when she wears prescription glasses. Thus, it must be that without those prescription glasses, she would demonstrate a lower level of visual acuity.

11. Plumb-Ace advertises that its plumbers are more qualified than plumbers at any other major plumbing firm in the region because Plumb-Ace plumbers must complete a very difficult certification process. Plumb-Ace plumbers may or may not be more qualified, but clearly the certification process is not very difficult, because nearly everyone who takes the written portion of the certification exam passes it very easily.

The reasoning in the argument is flawed in that it

(A) treats something that is necessary to make a certification process very difficult as if it were sufficient by itself to make the process very difficult

(B) takes for granted that plumbers are not qualified unless they complete some certification process

(C) overlooks the possibility that plumbers at other firms in the region complete certification processes that are even easier than that completed by Plumb-Ace's plumbers

(D) infers that a claim is false on the grounds that an inadequate argument has been given for that claim

(E) presumes that since one part of a whole lacks a certain characteristic, the whole must lack that characteristic as well

12. Historian: The early Egyptian pharaohs spent as much wealth on largely ceremonial and hugely impressive architecture as they did on roads and irrigation systems. This was not mere frivolousness, however, for if people under a pharaoh's rule could be made to realize the extent of their ruler's mastery of the physical world, their loyalty could be maintained without military coercion.

The claim that early Egyptian expenditure on largely ceremonial architecture was not frivolous plays which one of the following roles in the historian's argument?

(A) It is a conclusion purportedly justified by the argument's appeal to the psychological effects of these structures on the Egyptian population.

(B) It is offered in support of the claim that Egyptian pharaohs spent as much on ceremonial architecture as they did on roads and irrigation systems.

(C) It is a premise given in support of the claim that the loyalty of people under a pharaoh's rule was maintained over time without reliance on military force.

(D) It is offered as an illustration of the principle that social and political stability do not depend ultimately on force.

(E) It is a premise used to justify the pharaohs' policy of spending scarce resources on structures that have only military utility.

13. The proposed change to the patent system is bound to have a chilling effect on scientific research. Under current rules, researchers have one full year after the initial publication of a new discovery to patent the discovery. This allows research results to be shared widely prior to the patent application. The proposed change would have the application precede initial publication, which would delay the communication of discoveries.

The conclusion drawn above follows logically if which one of the following is assumed?

(A) The proposed change will encourage more patent applications to be filed.

(B) Dramatic advances in scientific research have occurred while the current patent system has been in place.

(C) Delays in the communication of discoveries will have a chilling effect on scientific research.

(D) Most researchers oppose the proposed change to the patent system.

(E) The current rules for patent applications facilitate progress in scientific research by rewarding the communication of discoveries.

GO ON TO THE NEXT PAGE.

14. Every time people get what they want they feel pleasure. Pleasure is a natural result of getting what one wants. We can conclude that no one fundamentally desires anything except pleasure.

Which one of the following uses questionable reasoning most similar to that used in the argument above?

(A) I sure am enjoying the party even though I was sure I would not, so I guess I wanted to come after all.

(B) I have never been skiing, but just thinking about it terrifies me, so I guess I must not want to learn how.

(C) Every time I eat pizza I get a stomachache, so I suppose the reason I eat pizza in the first place is so that I can have a stomachache.

(D) Every time I have gone to a party with Julio I have enjoyed myself, so I expect I will enjoy myself if Julio and I go to a party tonight.

(E) I never enjoy a soccer game without eating hot dogs, so I guess I would not enjoy going to a basketball game if I could not eat hot dogs at the game.

15. Linguist: You philosophers say that we linguists do not have a deep understanding of language, but you have provided no evidence.

Philosopher: Well, you have said that you believe that "Joan and Ivan are siblings" is identical in meaning to "Ivan and Joan are siblings." But this cannot be the case, for the sentences are physically different; yet for two things to be identical, they must have all the same attributes.

Of the following, which one is the strongest logical counter that the linguist can make to the philosopher?

(A) Two things can have a few minor differences and still be identical.

(B) Two sentences can be identical physically, and yet, depending on the context in which they are uttered, not be identical in meaning.

(C) It is necessarily true that Joan is Ivan's sibling if Ivan is Joan's sibling.

(D) The issue is not whether the two sentences are completely identical, but whether they mean the same thing.

(E) A linguist has more experience with language than a philosopher, and so is in a better position to answer such questions.

16. Salespeople always steer customers toward products from which they make their highest commissions, and all salespeople in major health stores work on commission. Hence, when you buy vitamin supplements in a major health store, you can be sure that the claims the salespeople make about the quality of the products are inaccurate.

The reasoning in the argument is flawed in that the argument

(A) offers as a premise a claim that merely paraphrases the conclusion and for which no support is provided

(B) infers that some claims are inaccurate solely on the basis of the source of those claims

(C) infers that just because a group of people has a certain property, each member of the group has that property

(D) takes a condition that is sufficient for the conclusion to be true as one that is necessary for the conclusion to be true

(E) relies on the claims of an authority on a topic outside that authority's area of expertise

GO ON TO THE NEXT PAGE.

17. Because no other theory has been able to predict it so simply and accurately, the advance of the perihelion of Mercury is sometimes cited as evidence in support of Einstein's theory of general relativity. However, this phenomenon was already well known when Einstein developed his theory, and he quite probably adjusted his equations to generate the correct numbers for the perihelion advance. Therefore, accounting for this advance should not be counted as evidence in support of Einstein's theory.

Which one of the following principles, if valid, most helps to justify the argument above?

(A) Unless a phenomenon predicted by a scientific theory is unknown at the time the theory is developed, the theory should not be credited with the discovery of that phenomenon.

(B) A phenomenon that is predicted by a scientific theory should not count as evidence in favor of that theory unless the theory was developed with that phenomenon in mind.

(C) Unless a theory can accurately account for all relevant phenomena that are already well known at the time of its development, it cannot be regarded as well supported.

(D) If a theory is adjusted specifically to account for some particular phenomenon, a match between that theory and that phenomenon should not count as evidence in favor of the theory.

(E) If a theory is adjusted to generate the correct predictions for some phenomenon that is already known to the scientist developing the theory, the theory should not be counted as predicting that phenomenon.

18. Computer store manager: Last year we made an average of 13 percent profit on the high-end computer models—those priced over $1,000—that we sold, while low-end models—those priced below $1,000—typically returned at least 25 percent profit. Since there is a limit to how many models we can display and sell, we should sell only low-end models. This would maximize our profits, since we would probably sell as many low-end models if that is all we sold as we would sell both kinds combined if we continued to sell both.

The reasoning in the manager's argument is vulnerable to criticism on which one of the following grounds?

(A) The argument fails to consider the possibility that the money earned on each high-end computer is significantly higher than the money earned on each low-end computer.

(B) The argument fails to address the possibility that, despite the price differential, the store sold as many high-end models as low-end models last year.

(C) The argument ignores the possibility that some customers who come into a computer store expecting to purchase a low-end model end up purchasing a high-end model.

(D) The argument presumes, without providing justification, that the sole objective in managing the computer store should be maximizing profits.

(E) The argument fails to recognize that future sales of low-end computers may not be the same as past sales.

GO ON TO THE NEXT PAGE.

19. Professor: Economists argue that buying lottery tickets is an unwise use of resources, because the average payoff for the tickets sold in a lottery is much lower than the cost of a ticket. But this reasoning is faulty. The average amount paid out on individual insurance policies is much lower than the average cost of a policy, yet nobody would argue that purchasing insurance is an unwise use of resources.

Which one of the following, if true, most weakens the professor's argument?

(A) Individuals spend, on average, much more on insurance than on lottery tickets.

(B) Insurance companies generally retain a higher proportion of total revenue than do organizations that sponsor lotteries.

(C) Taking small financial risks can often greatly increase one's chances of obtaining much larger benefits.

(D) In general, the odds of winning the grand prize in a lottery are significantly lower than the odds of collecting a settlement from a typical insurance policy.

(E) The protection against loss that insurance provides is more important to one's well-being than is the possibility of a windfall gain.

20. Unusually large and intense forest fires swept the tropics in 1997. The tropics were quite susceptible to fire at that time because of the widespread drought caused by an unusually strong El Niño, an occasional global weather phenomenon. Many scientists believe the strength of the El Niño was enhanced by the global warming caused by air pollution.

Which one of the following can be properly inferred from the information above?

(A) Air pollution was largely responsible for the size and intensity of the forest fires that swept the tropics in 1997.

(B) If the El Niño in 1997 had not been unusually strong, few if any large and intense forest fires would have swept the tropics in that year.

(C) Forest fires in the tropics are generally larger and more intense than usual during a strong El Niño.

(D) At least some scientists believe that air pollution was responsible for the size and intensity of the forest fires that swept the tropics in 1997.

(E) If air pollution enhanced the strength of the El Niño in 1997, then it also contributed to the widespread drought in that year.

21. If Skiff's book is published this year, Professor Nguyen vows she will urge the dean to promote Skiff. Thus, if Skiff's book is as important and as well written as Skiff claims, he will be promoted, for Nguyen will certainly keep her promise, and the dean will surely promote Skiff if Nguyen recommends it.

The argument's conclusion can be properly inferred if which one of the following is assumed?

(A) Skiff's book will be published this year if it is as important as he claims it is.

(B) Skiff needs to publish a book before he can be promoted.

(C) Professor Nguyen believes that Skiff's book is well written.

(D) Skiff's book will not be published unless it is as important and as well written as he claims it is.

(E) Skiff will not be promoted unless Professor Nguyen urges the dean to do so.

22. If the magazine's circulation continues to rise as it has over the last ten years, in another ten years it will be the largest-selling martial arts magazine in the world. Unfortunately, it has now become clear that the magazine's publisher will not allow the managing editor to make the changes she has proposed, and without these changes, the magazine's circulation will not rise as quickly over the next ten years as it has over the last ten. So the magazine will not be the largest-selling martial arts magazine ten years from now.

The argument's reasoning is flawed because the argument

(A) identifies some changes required for the magazine's circulation to continue its rapid increase and concludes from this that no other changes are needed

(B) equates a reduction in the rate at which the magazine's circulation is increasing with a decline in the magazine's circulation

(C) draws a conclusion that simply restates a claim that is presented in support of that conclusion

(D) takes a single fact that is incompatible with a general claim as enough to show that claim to be false

(E) treats an occurrence that will ensure a certain outcome as something that is required for that outcome

GO ON TO THE NEXT PAGE.

23. Botanist: In an experiment, scientists raised domesticated radishes in a field with wild radishes, which are considered weeds. Within several generations, the wild radishes began to show the same flower color as the domesticated ones. This suggests that resistance to pesticides, which is often a genetically engineered trait, would also be passed from domesticated crop plants to their relatives that are considered weeds.

Which one of the following, if true, most strengthens the botanist's argument?

(A) It is much easier in principle for genetic traits to be passed from wild plants to their domesticated relatives than it is for such traits to be passed from the domesticated plant to the wild relative.

(B) When the ratio of domesticated radishes to wild radishes in the field increased, the speed with which the flower color passed to the wild radishes also increased.

(C) Radishes are not representative of crop plants in general with respect to the ease with which various traits are passed among members of closely related species.

(D) The flower color of the domesticated radishes had not been introduced into them via genetic engineering.

(E) It is more difficult for flower color to be transferred between domesticated and wild radishes than it is for almost any other trait to be passed between any two similarly related plant species.

24. Parents who consistently laud their children for every attempt to accomplish something, whether successful or not, actually erode the youngsters' sense of self-esteem. Children require commendation for their achievements, but if uniformly praised for both what they have accomplished and what they have merely attempted, they will eventually discount all words of commendation. In effect, such children never hear any praise at all.

Which one of the following most accurately expresses the overall conclusion of the argument?

(A) Parents should praise their children for their achievements.

(B) Children whose actions are praised undeservedly eventually learn to discount all words of praise.

(C) Parents need to distinguish between their own expectations for their children and what their children are actually capable of accomplishing.

(D) Children's self-esteem will suffer if their parents uniformly praise their attempts to accomplish things regardless of their success or failure.

(E) Children will develop low self-esteem if their parents do not praise them when they succeed.

25. Pauline: Some environmentalists claim that for the salmon to be saved, the hydroelectric dams on the river must be breached. But if the dams are breached, given the region's growing population and booming industry, electrical costs will skyrocket.

Roger: The dams are already producing electricity at optimal capacity. So regardless of whether they are breached, we will have to find additional energy sources for the region.

The dialogue provides the most support for the claim that Pauline and Roger agree that

(A) production from other energy sources cannot be increased in the near future to compensate for electricity production lost by breaching the dams

(B) there will be no significant decrease in demand for electricity in the region in the near future

(C) if the dams remain in service but do not operate at optimal capacity, electrical costs in the region will rise

(D) some environmentalists who advocate saving the salmon believe that that goal overrides concerns about electrical costs

(E) finding additional energy sources will not decrease the electrical costs in the region

S T O P

IF YOU FINISH BEFORE TIME IS CALLED, YOU MAY CHECK YOUR WORK ON THIS SECTION ONLY.
DO NOT WORK ON ANY OTHER SECTION IN THE TEST.

Acknowledgment is made to the following sources from which material has been adapted for use in this test booklet:

Timothy B. Lee, "Vonage Is the Latest Victim of Patent Abuse." ©2007 by The American. http://www.american.com/archive/2007/april-0407/vonage-is-the-latest-victim-of-patent-abuse.

David Quammen, *The Song of the Dodo: Island Biography in an Age of Extinctions*. ©1996 by David Quammen.

Red Hat, Inc., "Statement of Position and Our Promise on Software Patents." ©2007 by Red Hat, Inc. http://www.redhat.com/legal/patent_policy.html.

Lyle Rexer, "Photographers Move Forward into the Past." ©1998 by The New York Times Company.

Booker T. Whatley, *How to Make $100,000 Farming 25 Acres*. ©1987 by the Regenerative Agriculture Association.

Wait for the supervisor's instructions before you open the page to the topic.
Please print and sign your name and write the date in the designated spaces below.

Time: 35 Minutes

General Directions

You will have 35 minutes in which to plan and write an essay on the topic inside. Read the topic and the accompanying directions carefully. You will probably find it best to spend a few minutes considering the topic and organizing your thoughts before you begin writing. In your essay, be sure to develop your ideas fully, leaving time, if possible, to review what you have written. **Do not write on a topic other than the one specified. Writing on a topic of your own choice is not acceptable.**

No special knowledge is required or expected for this writing exercise. Law schools are interested in the reasoning, clarity, organization, language usage, and writing mechanics displayed in your essay. How well you write is more important than how much you write.

Confine your essay to the blocked, lined area on the front and back of the separate Writing Sample Response Sheet. Only that area will be reproduced for law schools. Be sure that your writing is legible.

Both this topic sheet and your response sheet must be turned in to the testing staff before you leave the room.

Topic Code	Print Your Full Name Here		
117141	Last	First	M.I.

Date	Sign Your Name Here
/ /	

Scratch Paper
Do not write your essay in this space.

LSAT® Writing Sample Topic

> Directions: The scenario presented below describes two choices, either one of which can be supported on the basis of the information given. Your essay should consider both choices and argue for one over the other, based on the two specified criteria and the facts provided. There is no "right" or "wrong" choice: a reasonable argument can be made for either.

WildCare, a donor-supported organization that rescues and rehabilitates injured or sick wild animals, currently rents a portion of the facility that houses the local animal shelter. WildCare is deciding whether to stay where it is or relocate to a new facility. Using the facts below, write an essay in which you argue for one option over the other based on the following two criteria:

- WildCare's mission is to provide the highest quality care to the greatest number of animals.
- WildCare wants to maintain a strong donor base.

The building that houses both the animal shelter and WildCare is located in town, where it is easily accessible to both the local community and the surrounding region. WildCare is often able to borrow supplies such as cages, heating pads, and towels from the animal shelter. Most of WildCare's donors and volunteers learn of WildCare through interactions with the animal shelter. There is friction between WildCare and the building management over WildCare's need for upgraded electrical and water services and its desire to house more animals on the grounds. WildCare has foundation grants for supplies and staff support that are contingent on its remaining in the town.

At the new location WildCare would be the only occupant of a freestanding building adjacent to a nature preserve. An environmental education organization hosts a variety of wildlife-oriented activities for the public at the preserve. The director of the nature preserve would like WildCare to relocate there and has offered assistance with the move. Several of WildCare's larger donors are supportive of the move. The location is some distance from the town and is difficult to reach. There would be room to house more animals.

WP-U117A

Scratch Paper
Do not write your essay in this space.

Writing Sample Response Sheet

DO NOT WRITE IN THIS SPACE

**Begin your essay in the lined area below.
Continue on the back if you need more space.**

COMPUTING YOUR SCORE

Directions:

1. Use the Answer Key on the next page to check your answers.

2. Use the Scoring Worksheet below to compute your raw score.

3. Use the Score Conversion Chart to convert your raw score into the 120–180 scale.

Scoring Worksheet

1. Enter the number of questions you answered correctly in each section.

	Number Correct
SECTION I.................	_____
SECTION II................	_____
SECTION III...............	_____
SECTION IV	_____

2. Enter the sum here: _____

This is your Raw Score.

Conversion Chart
For Converting Raw Score to the 120–180 LSAT Scaled Score
LSAT Form 4LSN106

Reported Score	Raw Score Lowest	Raw Score Highest
180	98	100
179	*	*
178	97	97
177	96	96
176	95	95
175	94	94
174	93	93
173	92	92
172	91	91
171	90	90
170	89	89
169	87	88
168	86	86
167	84	85
166	83	83
165	81	82
164	80	80
163	78	79
162	76	77
161	74	75
160	73	73
159	71	72
158	69	70
157	67	68
156	65	66
155	63	64
154	62	62
153	60	61
152	58	59
151	56	57
150	54	55
149	52	53
148	51	51
147	49	50
146	47	48
145	45	46
144	44	44
143	42	43
142	40	41
141	39	39
140	37	38
139	36	36
138	34	35
137	33	33
136	31	32
135	30	30
134	29	29
133	28	28
132	26	27
131	25	25
130	24	24
129	23	23
128	22	22
127	21	21
126	20	20
125	19	19
124	*	*
123	18	18
122	16	17
121	*	*
120	0	15

*There is no raw score that will produce this scaled score for this form.

ANSWER KEY

SECTION I

1.	B	8.	C	15.	C	22.	B
2.	A	9.	A	16.	D	23.	A
3.	D	10.	D	17.	C	24.	C
4.	D	11.	E	18.	E	25.	B
5.	C	12.	E	19.	E		
6.	A	13.	B	20.	B		
7.	B	14.	A	21.	C		

SECTION II

1.	E	8.	C	15.	A	22.	D
2.	A	9.	B	16.	D	23.	B
3.	E	10.	C	17.	B		
4.	C	11.	A	18.	D		
5.	D	12.	A	19.	E		
6.	B	13.	D	20.	A		
7.	E	14.	C	21.	C		

SECTION III

1.	A	8.	A	15.	C	22.	B
2.	B	9.	B	16.	B	23.	A
3.	C	10.	E	17.	E	24.	D
4.	A	11.	C	18.	B	25.	A
5.	D	12.	D	19.	A	26.	E
6.	D	13.	B	20.	D	27.	C
7.	B	14.	A	21.	D		

SECTION IV

1.	E	8.	C	15.	D	22.	E
2.	D	9.	B	16.	B	23.	E
3.	B	10.	B	17.	D	24.	D
4.	B	11.	E	18.	A	25.	B
5.	E	12.	A	19.	E		
6.	D	13.	C	20.	E		
7.	E	14.	C	21.	A		

LSAT® PREP TOOLS

New! The Official LSAT Handbook™

Get to know the LSAT

The LSAT is a test of Analytical Reasoning, Logical Reasoning, and Reading Comprehension, including Comparative Reading. What's the best way to learn how to approach these types of questions *before* you encounter them on the day of the test? There's no better way than The Official LSAT Handbook, published by the Law School Admission Council, the organization that produces the LSAT. This inexpensive guide will introduce you to the skills that the LSAT is designed to assess so that you can make the most of the rest of your test preparation and do your best on the test. (Note: This handbook contains information that is also included in The Official LSAT SuperPrep®. The information in The Official LSAT Handbook has been expanded and updated since it was first published in The Official LSAT SuperPrep.)

$12 online

LSAC.org